BALLS
TO FLY

AN AUTOBIOGRAPHY

RICKY ELLCOCK

fairfield books

BALLS TO FLY

AN AUTOBIOGRAPHY

First published by Fairfield Books in 2023

fairfield books

Fairfield Books
Bedser Stand
Kia Oval
London
SE11 5SS

Typeset in Garamond, BBC Raith Sans XBold and Proxima Nova
Typesetting by Rob Whitehouse
Cover by Joe Provis

A CIP catalogue record for is available from the British Library

Printed by CPI Group (UK) Ltd

The greatest glory in living lies not in never falling, but in rising every time we fall.

Nelson Mandela

CONTENTS

MY MUM, THE POPE

I once joked with 'The Pope' that I would get the organist at her funeral to play 'Going Underground' by The Jam. She did not think it was very funny.

After her passing, we found she had over 60 hats. Instead of calling her The Pope, we should have called her Imelda Marcos…

My mum had always said she did not want a eulogy or flowers after her death. She would say, "Tell me what you want to say while I am alive, so I can hear you. And give me the flowers while I am living so I can smell them." With that in mind, this is a thank you, not a eulogy.

Born a pure left-hander, the only thing my mum did right-handed was writing, and that was because in 1930s, 40s and 50s Barbados, to be born left-handed made you a witch, and so it was beaten out of you. And by the way, what beautiful handwriting.

My brother and I played 'Test matches' in the backyard that lasted for weeks, and if one of us batted for too long, Pope would often have a spell of bowling. Left-arm over or round, and you'd better not be on the front foot too early or you would be greeted with the odd beamer!

Pope was born on 16 June 1946 into a working-class background, which meant she and my dad expected to be given nothing. Two examples of this. When I was a 12-year-old at Combermere School, my dad asked me what I wanted to be when I was older. I instantly said a pilot. His reply was that black people do not fly aeroplanes, and had I thought about medicine, law or engineering? That, of course, made me want to fly even more. Years later, I said to my mum, "You have worked as a maid at Ready-Mix for such a long time, do you not think you should have been promoted by now?" She said, "What in God's earth madness are you talking?" That shows the difference in modern-day expectations and those of black people of the 1930s and 1940s.

She was the bravest person I have ever met. Can you imagine in the early 1980s two white men turning up at your door and saying to you, "Your son has a very special talent, and we would like to take him to England."? I know what I would have said.

But after her due diligence, she said yes, and I went off to one of the best boarding schools in the world, costing £45,000 a year in today's money, a sum that would have taken her two lifetimes to earn. That is why I am in the position I am in today. As they say in *Top Gun*, "Gutsiest move I ever saw, Pope."

I feel blessed that I was able to take her all over the world. From Seattle to San Francisco, Las Vegas to Los Angeles, New York to South Africa. I once advised her to choose expensive items at the buffet at the Bellagio in Vegas. When she returned with bacon and eggs, I said, "Mum, you can have that in Barbados anytime." Her reply, "Ricky, why don't you get on with your business and let me get on with mine."

Our relationship could, be fiery. I suppose that's inevitable when your 11-year-old, who has only just passed for Combermere School, comes home with dreadlocks and an earring.

In a different era, I firmly believe she would have been a Combermere girl. She was extremely intelligent but not a bookworm; it was her I would ask to spell words, and she was way better at maths than me. She was argumentative but not overbearing, a visionary, brave, multi-dimensional, social, liked a drink in the right circumstances, and above all she was fiercely loyal to her inner circle.

Pope was very proud of me, as I was of her. She could discuss the hydraulic system of a 747 and had an encyclopaedic knowledge of Virgin Atlantic flight schedules. I often relied on her for my departure times!

On learning of my mum's death, Lisa, who worked as cabin crew, phoned to give her sympathy and tell me she had met my mum before she ever met me. I said, how? She said., "I was serving your mum on a Barbados flight, and she said to me, 'My son is a captain on this airline and on this aircraft.' I thought she was confused because I knew we did not have any black pilots, and then, of course, I flew with you years later!" She told everyone about me.

Mum, I want to say thank you from the bottom of my heart for always being there for me.

A few years ago, when I was gravely ill, Pope dropped everything, flew to England and spent a month (literally) at my bedside. Every day she navigated the London Underground. At 10am, when the ward opened, in she walked. And at 10pm, it closed, off she went.

I have eaten my last coucou, no more buljol on landing day, no point in flying my pilot shirts from London to be washed in Barbados. And I will never again hear you say, "The end is near", "Life is not fair" or "Why don't you get on with your business and let me get on with mine?".

COMBERMERE SCHOOL SONG

Up and On

Lives are in the making here
Hearts are in the waking here
Mighty undertaking here
Up and on, up and on.

We are arming for the fight
Pressing on with all our might
Pluming wings for higher flight
Up and on, up and on.

Up then! Truest fame lies in high endeavour
Play the game, keep the flame burning brightly ever
Up then! Truest fame lies in high endeavour
Play the game, keep the flame burning brightly ever

Foes in plenty we shall meet
Hearts courageous scorn defeat
So we press with eager feet
Up and on, up and on.
Ever upward to the fight
Ever upward to the light
Ever true to God and Right
Up and on, up and on.

Fair before us lies the way
Time for work and time for play
Fill the measure while we may
Up and on, up and on.
Life and time will not delay
Time is running fast away
Life is now – today, today
Up and on, up and on.

John Oxenham

FOREWORD

In the world of cricket, there are individuals whose stories transcend the boundaries of the field, weaving a narrative that inspires, astonishes, and captures the very essence of the sport.

Ricky Ellcock is undeniably one of those exceptional souls. I have had the privilege of standing alongside Ricky on the hallowed grounds of both Lord's and countless other cricketing arenas, representing England and Middlesex County Cricket Club.

Our journeys as team-mates were marked by camaraderie, fierce competition, and countless shared moments of triumph and defeat. These experiences have shaped my perspective on cricket, but none more so than the indomitable spirit of Ricky Ellcock.

As you turn the pages of this autobiography, you will discover the remarkable trajectory of a man who rose from humble beginnings to become a cricketing legend. Ricky's story is not only a testament to his extraordinary talent with bat and ball but also a reflection of the resilience and determination that define his character.

His journey takes us from the dusty fields of his youth to the grandeur of international cricket, offering an intimate look at the sacrifices and struggles he faced along the way. You will gain insight into the discipline, the sweat, and the unyielding passion that forged a formidable cricketer out of a young dreamer.

But Ricky's tale is not just about cricket. It's a narrative of family, friendship, and the values that guided him through the highs and lows of life in the cricketing world. It's a reminder that the true essence of the game lies in the bonds we create, the stories we share, and the legacy we leave behind.

As I reflect on our shared experiences, I am reminded of the countless hours spent on the field, the joy of victory, and the agony of defeat. But most of all, I am struck by the remarkable journey of a man who, through his autobiography, invites us to witness a life lived in pursuit of a dream, a passion, and a love for the game.

Ricky's autobiography is a testament to his remarkable career and an embodiment of the values and aspirations that cricket holds dear. It's a story of triumph over adversity, of dreams fulfilled and ambitions achieved. It's a celebration of a cricketer who has left an indelible mark on the sport, as well as on the hearts of those fortunate enough to share the field with him.

So, as you embark on this literary journey, I encourage you to immerse yourself in the life and times of Ricky Ellcock, a cricketer whose name will forever be etched in the annals of the game. This is a tale of dedication, perseverance, and an unwavering love for cricket. It is my honour to introduce you to the man, the teammate, and the friend I have had the privilege of knowing, learning from, and sharing the joys of cricket with – Ricky Ellcock. Enjoy the journey.

Roland Butcher
Middlesex CCC and England

INTRODUCTION

Born into abject poverty on an idyllic Caribbean island, less than a mile from the exclusive £10,000-a-night Sandy Lane Hotel, the PGA golf course and the multi-million-pound houses on the west coast of Barbados. Grew up in a two-room wooden hut with no kitchen, toilet or running water. Remembers his mum crying her eyes out because she could not afford to buy him and his brother an ice cream.

A sickly child, clever enough to gain entry into one of the Caribbean's most prestigious secondary schools, following in the footsteps of heads of Government, scholars and great sportsmen.

A child prodigy at cricket who gained a scholarship to one of England's most prestigious boarding schools and would mix with royalty and the kids of the rich and famous. As a teenager there, had to deal with the intricacies of a British boarding school, politics, weather and society. And being homesick.

Made his first-class cricket debut as a 17-year-old while still at school and was selected to play for England as a 24-year-old, but his career would ultimately end in disaster with a back injury.

Two major, unsuccessful operations ended that career, driving him into bouts of severe depression and the need to rebuild his life.

Armed with the determination to prove his dad wrong, after he had told him as a 12-year-old, 'black people don't fly airplanes' and short of funds, he set off for flight school and a highly challenging academic period.

After flight school and the challenges of getting an airline job as one of the few black pilots in England, a chance encounter led to a job at Virgin Atlantic. There, he had to bear the weight of being their first black pilot, rising through the ranks.

Dealt with the scourge of prejudice and racism that continued through boarding school, cricket, flying, and now parenting his son.

Having got to the top of his second profession, disaster struck and a fall brought him to the brink of death on four separate occasions. Suffered further depression, rebuilt a life, and tried to prevent another career ending.

On the road to recovery, feeling he had seen the worst of life, suffered and another kick in the balls – the death of the one person who had kept him grounded, stable and had stood by him all his life.

Why him? Why Ricky Ellcock?

CHAPTER 1

FLYING HOME

It's the beginning of January 1997. My wife, Kate, phones with good news.

'Virgin Atlantic Airways have offered you an interview in February.'

The rush is on. All my annual leave has been used up attending the birth of my son Isaac the October before.

I have limited time to get to England and learn about the Virgin Atlantic interview process. As luck would have it, the manager of my mum's workplace is married to the sister of a Virgin Atlantic captain. Geoffrey Patterson, a white Barbadian, schooled at Harrison College, started his flying career at the Barbados Light Airplane Club. He trained at the Oxford Air Training School before flying for Tropic Air, Caricargo, Laker Airways, Cal Air, Novair and now Virgin Atlantic Airways. He advises me that the process comprises a technical questionnaire, psychometric test, interview ...

... and a 747-simulator check!

Wow!

The biggest aeroplane I have flown is the twin-engine 37-seat Dash 8. The 747 is a partial double-decker with four engines and accommodates 400 passengers. To fly this simulator without any previous knowledge will be a challenge.

Getting the time off to attend the interview is proving difficult at short notice. My colleague and training partner, Richie Kangoo, comes to the rescue. He offers to work as much of my roster as possible, tries to swap the other flights for me, and if all else fails, he will call in sick on my behalf – a noble gesture that puts both of our jobs at risk but will help me progress my career!

Soon I find a 747-simulator for hire, located at the TWA training facility at JFK. I book a two-hour slot. Getting myself to New York and onto London will be tricky; with me bunking off work, I cannot use the regional airline LIAT's staff travel. So, Richie and I devise a plan for me to get to Barbados and request a jump-seat ride with the 'BeeWee' [BWIA – British West Indian Airlines] crew operating BGI-JFK. This way, my movement will be untraceable. Two hours in the B747 simulator and then an overnight flight, I arrive in London the day before my interview. I'm tired, and it is difficult with a young baby in the house, but I'm determined not to miss my interview.

I journey to Virgin Atlantic Flight Centre in Horley with constant butterflies in my stomach. The order of the day is the psychometric test, technical questionnaire, followed by an interview with a panel, and then group discussions. If it goes well, the simulator check will be scheduled for the following week. This will be problematic, as Richie is only expecting to cover a few days of flying.

The panel comprises three members: Malcolm Wagstaff, Director of Operations; Nicole Svatek, Head of HR; and captain George Newby, Head of the 747-400 fleet. The questions are about my educational background, previous employment, and cricketing career. I begin to feel comfortable. I feel it's gone quite well.

Interview over, we are joined by several Virgin Atlantic staff. I'm keen to talk to as many pilots as possible. Captain Newby arrives and comes over for a chat.

'Where in Barbados are you from?'

'Do you know Barbados quite well, sir?' I ask.

'Yes, my wife is Bajan, and I have a Barbados passport.'

Wow, what a coincidence. Maybe this is the luck I need.

Soon, a phone call from Virgin Atlantic comes...

I have made it through the interview and am offered a simulator date in a week! This is pushing Richie's ingenuity at roster manipulation to the absolute maximum.

Captain Dave Curties is the simulator check captain, in a giant warehouse on a giant industrial estate full of giant spiders. The cockpit is not alien; a couple of hours in the TWA simulator has proven helpful. The programme will be conducted at Heathrow and comprises all types of approaches. The visual approaches should play to my strengths after operating in the Caribbean. As we descend towards the runway visually, captain Curties freezes the simulator at intervals and asks, 'Where do you think you are, high, low, or in the slot?' Each time I'm in the slot.

Kate phones with the great news within a few days of returning to Antigua. Virgin Atlantic has offered me a second officer position on the 747-400, based at London Heathrow, starting 8 May 1997. LIAT is proving bloody-minded, however. If I'm unable to work my entire notice period, they are threatening to withhold my Provident Fund and reference. My Provident Fund is approximately 12,000EC dollars, and although I'm loath to give it up, I might have to.

However, there is no way around the withholding of a reference. And so, I decide to discuss the situation with LIAT chief examiner Ferdi Degannes, who has always favoured young pilots progressing their careers. Ferdi is excited for me and feels this is an opportunity not to be missed. Accordingly, he asks that the reference request be sent directly to him.

On the morning of 8 May 1997, the butterflies are back. There are four of us joining today: the Aussie, Mark Fry, the English pair of Nick Taylor, Gary Oakley, and myself. We are divided into pairs; Gary will be my training partner for the duration of the course. The flight centre in Horley will be our base for the next four weeks. The exam will be taken at the CAA office next door to Gatwick Airport. It is a building I remember well, having taken over 20 exams there as a flight student. It was known to us as 'the Kremlin'. Second officer course completed and, after two years flying, I progress to first officer training.

Captain Lefort will be the operating pilot back to Heathrow, and having avoided any major mistakes on the outbound leg, I feel relatively confident. Having arrived back at Heathrow, test completed, I have passed. I'm now a first officer and graduate to wearing two bars on my shoulder and jacket sleeves instead of the one-and-a-half bar of the second officer uniform. My next promotion will be in two years to senior first officer, wearing three bars. From now on, the hard work begins towards the ultimate goal, 'Command' of a wide-body aircraft. Every test and every check-ride will count.

With Virgin Atlantic expanding rapidly, and several new routes and aircraft, many commanders are needed. Every first officer in the company is deep in the manuals in preparation for what promises to be the most exhaustive test of a pilot's aviation knowledge. The 'Widebody Command Course'.

9 September 2001, the return leg of my first flight as a senior first officer. We arrive at Logan Airport Boston and can see the aircraft parked behind the check-in desk. It's G-VROY, Virgin's newest aircraft and one of five ordered by Alitalia, but with the Italian airline in financial trouble, they have cancelled the order. With the expansion

of Virgin Atlantic, the management has opted to take delivery of the total cancelled order.

We land back at Heathrow on the morning of 10 September. I have lost a whole night's sleep. I try to remain awake to spend some time with Isaac. Being off tomorrow, I can sleep late before continuing my studying.

The morning of 11 September 2001, I'm awoken by the phone, 'Shit, I have overslept.' It is after midday. My mate Alan has called to tell me a plane has hit the World Trade Centre. My first impression is how could you hit something that size. It must be a student pilot lost in the New York area. Alan shouts, 'Shit, another one has hit it!' It is a co-ordinated terrorist attack by suicide bombers who have hijacked four airliners. By the end of the day, the two towers of the World Trade Centre have been demolished, and over 3,000 people have died. Aviation and aviation security have changed forever.

Following the 11 September attacks, the industry is in dire straits, with several airlines going bankrupt, filing for bankruptcy protection, cancelling flights and grounding aircraft. My first flight after the terrorist attacks is the VIR19 to San Francisco on 18 September. It is a sombre flight; for an aircraft capable of carrying 450 passengers, the load is just 25. Virgin Atlantic Airways' primary market is the USA; if this slump continues, it will be difficult to survive.

We arrive back in England to the news that Virgin Atlantic has grounded their entire 747-200 fleet and made all the pilots that fly it redundant. This is a massive shock as major airlines have historically operated a seniority-based system, which means last in, first out. Virgin Atlantic has three aircraft types and has decided against retraining any 747-200 pilots. This is terrible news for all first officers of my seniority, expecting an imminent promotion. The one positive for me is that with the 747-200 grounded, the Caribbean will now be served by the 747-400.

As the first two Barbadian-born pilots in Virgin Atlantic, captain Geoffrey Patterson and myself are rostered to operate the inaugural 747-400, London Gatwick-Barbados flight on 4 October 2001. There is a stark contrast between the American flights I have done since 11 September and this flight. It is full, with the passengers smiling and looking forward to their holiday. Geoff is the flying pilot, and I'm operating the radios. From Geoff's first PA, passengers have detected this is not the typical British accent.

'Gatwick ground Virgin 29 requesting push and start.'

'Confirm Virgin 29.'

As the flight progresses, several air traffic control centres want confirmation of the call sign. Piarco Control in Trinidad is bold enough not only to ask for call sign confirmation but to observe,

'You sound like you are from the islands.'

'I am,' I say, 'as a matter of fact, both of us up here are from the islands.'

The reply:

'Sweet.'

Our proudest moment is descending through flight level 290, calling Barbados air traffic control.

'Adams' control, Virgin 29 leaving flight level 290, descending flight level 250.'

'Confirm Virgin 29.'

'Yes, Virgin 29.'

'Confirm you are a Bajan.'

'There are two Bajans up here.'

'Excellent; welcome home to both of you.'

CHAPTER 2

IN THE BEGINNING

They say if you're going to make an entrance, make it a good one. Mine was certainly memorable, especially for Mum, who had endured a lengthy labour, delivering me one day after her 19th birthday. It was pretty special too for the residents of Redman's Village in Barbados, who would never pass up the opportunity of a good drink-up.

I was born on the morning of Thursday, 17 June 1965, at the Queen Elizabeth Hospital, weighing in at a healthy 8lb 6ozs. My parents hailed from neighbouring villages; mum, Marian Husbands, from Cave Hill, close to the university campus, and dad, Everson Ellcock, from Redman's Village, St Thomas. A good-looking man with a fast bicycle, dad was a major pull for the girls back in the 1960s. Nine years older than mum, he was a carpenter by trade, though he later worked as the head foreman at the National Housing Corporation. Not to be outdone, I'd made a noisy entrance at birth, apparently crying through most of my first day. I was still crying when my dad arrived to see me for the first time, though he couldn't have been any prouder of the new arrival. He brought a bag of fruit for Mum and was taken by Dr Singh, a trainee doing his house jobs, into a room full of screaming babies; he addressed the new parents, saying, 'I hope he grows up to be a doctor'. Proudly holding me in his arms, Dad knew he was in for a big drinking session when he returned to the village.

The story of dad's return to the village became legendary, as he headed back to tell everyone he 'didn't shoot blanks' and that he had 'lead in his pencil!' The celebrations continued late into the night, all having one 'on the baby's head'. This went on until Pearl, the shopkeeper, decided he wanted to get some sleep. To continue the session, everyone moved into Everson's house, a small two-bedroomed building with an outside bathroom and toilet. Chattel houses are modest dwellings that working-class people occupy – chattel is a slavery word, and as with cattle, means movable property. There is generally just one living area and a small kitchen attached, though much of the cooking would typically be done outside. There were some thick heads around that Friday morning, but it was back to work for Dad and then back to the hospital to hear that mum and baby were doing well, and that they'd be allowed home the following day. For someone who was never very good at housework, it meant Dad had to get his act together to get things ready. He was up nice and early on the Saturday morning to do the cleaning. After a shower, he got dressed in his smartest clothes. Denny Luke, a long-time friend, arrived with a spotless car, and the pair of them came to the hospital to collect Mum and me.

The drive back to the house was full of talk about parenthood. Mum sat in the back seat and chatted mainly in baby talk. Back at the house, it seemed the whole village had turned out to greet us, and everyone took turns holding me in their arms. I was named Ricardo McDonald Husbands and christened at St. Stephen's Protestant church in Black Rock, St. Michael. Husbands was my mum's maiden name, though Dad got his way with my other names; Ricardo was from an American screen actor he admired, Ricardo Montalban (famous for his roles in *Fantasy Island* and *Star Trek*), with McDonald being my dad's middle name. Over the next couple of years, I was the apple of my parents' eyes and received all the love and attention a growing toddler could ask for, even when times were hard. The only thing I didn't have at that time was a sibling. But that soon changed. Mum had secretly hoped for a girl but was pleased it was another healthy baby. She got half her way with naming this child: Dale Everson Husbands. Although a new arrival meant there was even less money, it did mean there was a passing down of clothes from the older son to his new brother. When the cash got shorter, and grandparents and uncles began chipping in, Mum, a fiercely independent person, decided she would get a job. This was not a proposition Dad was very happy about, with the West Indian male kicking in. However, Mum was determined and soon found a job, working a half-day job as a maid. This would mean Dale and I would spend the mornings with our neighbours, Eunice and Ossie Ellis (we found the name Eunice too difficult to pronounce, so we called her 'Haa'). At the age of four, I started my schooling at Welches Mixed school, located just on the edge of the village. It comprised six classes, Infants A&B, Class 1, 2, 3, and 4, each containing about 20 pupils, with the more gifted kids getting to sit the Common Entrance Exam for secondary education when they reached Class 3. I was initially a very reluctant scholar, with Mum spending many hours trying to convince me that school was worthwhile, even though she would have gladly kept me at home. That wasn't an option, and I agreed to go, with her coaxing. However, I had conditions. I agreed to attend school for that first term provided I could sit with one of the older boys, Harry Bruce, who lived across the road from us.

That same year Mum and dad got married and, a year later, our family unit was completed with the birth of my sister, Alison Cassandra (Mum finally got her way with the name); she was the first to take the Ellcock surname.

Life couldn't have been easy for our parents with three hungry mouths to feed, but we were always loved and provided for. Dale and I shared one bedroom, with Alison having a cot in with our parents. There would be challenges, of course. I remember a period when Dale was very poorly. He'd contracted bronchitis so severe that he had to be hospitalised for several weeks. This coincided with Barbados being hit by severe flooding, causing death and widespread damage and it meant a hazardous journey for Mum in her daily visits to the hospital. The floods gradually abated, and Dale recovered.

Family life was at the centre of everything, and I was fortunate that our close-knit community always ensured we were well looked after, with food in our bellies, even if money was scarce. Like most Bajan youngsters, I recall a childhood full of fun and adventure, with many mishaps and laughter. There was nearly always a game of bat and ball going on in the main street; indeed, we played various cricket games – tip and run, one-hand one-bounce, that sort of thing. Unfortunately, a proper bat and ball weren't often available, so we would improvise, with coconut tree branches as the bat, until Dad did some carving and made us some better ones! Mum's plastic fruit display also disappeared, with the apples, oranges, and pears put to good use as balls. When we got older, we'd cover a rock with a bicycle inner tube that'd been cut into strips. This then progressed to a tennis ball if we could find one. The street was pretty narrow, with many windows accidentally broken. On one or two occasions, the electric company had to reconnect the supply to the village though if anyone asks, it was never our fault.

Dad worked hard, and like most Bajan men, he enjoyed his downtime. He liked a drink and was also a massive fan of both cricket and horse racing. Indeed, he played cricket for the local team and always followed the progress of the West Indies side, usually via his little portable radio. That little Sony would eat batteries, and if I saw him put fresh batteries in once, I saw him do it a thousand times. If ever there was an exciting climax to a Test match, we'd all gather round the set, hanging on the commentator's words and cheering on the familiar names. Then there'd be shouting and complaining when the batteries needed changing again! When the West Indies were playing overseas, somewhere like Australia, India or Pakistan, I remember lying in bed and listening to it all unfold. Dad would occasionally take Dale and me to Welches to watch him play. I loved that, as I could run about and play with some of the other lads but would also keep an eye on the match and cheer whenever someone from Dad's side did well. There was one occasion when he obviously didn't want us there and said to come later with Mum. I wouldn't have been very old at this stage, perhaps five or six. Despite pleading with him, he refused, 'No, you stay here!' I was so upset I ran crying into the bedroom and threw myself on the bed. Unfortunately, I hit a mirror, which smashed and sliced into my leg, badly cutting it. I still have the scar.

Dad also enjoyed going to the races, being with his mates, discussing the horses, and having a drink and a bet. They would walk from one starting stall to the next, studying the form. This happened most Saturdays when there wasn't any cricket. Occasionally he'd take us with him but left us with a lady called Lolita, who had a food stall. He'd give us a dollar each for sweets, but knowing his boys would be hungry, he would ask Lolita to provide us with whatever we wanted, squaring his tab up at the end of the day.

The Kensington Oval is the epicentre of sporting life in Barbados. Finally, the day came when I was allowed to go for the first time. Dad obviously had a big day lined up with his mates because Mum also came and was left looking after us. It was a huge occasion, and everyone on the island was talking about it. To set the scene, Garfield Sobers, the most famous Barbadian (though Rihanna fans might debate this!), was involved in the final Test series of his long and illustrious playing career, against England in 1974, with his countrymen all wanting to give him a suitable send-off. The stadium was rammed full of people, and the atmosphere was electric. I remember we sat in the lower tier of the old double-decker stand, roughly where the pavilion is nowadays. Sobers may have brought the crowd in, but a Jamaican, Lawrence 'Yagga' Rowe, hogged the limelight, scoring a triple-century. It was a brilliant effort from Rowe, and that one innings elevated him to superstar status overnight. He added 249 with the little Guyanese left-hander, Alvin Kallicharran, whose own century almost seemed to go unnoticed. As I'll usually root for the underdog, I decided that from then on, Kallicharran would be my favourite cricketer. Another stand-out that long, hot day was my head on my mom's knee when a 50-cent coin fell from the upper deck into her lap. 'Oh,' she exclaimed, 'Money from heaven.'

I was always an academically gifted kid but mischievous and easily distracted. Primary schools in Barbados effectively cover three subjects: Maths, English and Comprehension. Since that throwaway comment from Dr Singh ('I hope he grows up to be a doctor'), mum had always seen it as my destiny to enter the medical profession, constantly reminding me that I needed to work a little harder in the classroom toward that goal. Worryingly, I soon experienced some medical problems of my own, missing several days at school due to nose bleeds. Doctors were summoned to find the problem, but none could. Worse, the Common Entrance Exam was fast approaching. An elderly EN&T doctor, Dr Reader, was recommended. He'd moved to the island from England and was happy to see me, once the fee had been mustered, of course! Fortunately, it was nothing more serious than a dust allergy, the good doctor adding I should soon grow out of it. As my exams drew closer, I was sent to a lady in the village, by the name of Myrtle, for some extra tuition. This would be another drain on the family's resources, but my parents were determined I should get high enough grades to meet the entrance requirements for one of the three best schools: Harrison's College, Lodge, or Combermere. Anything less wouldn't be deemed good enough, so opportunities for me to go out to play became scarce. Naturally, I resisted, and so the bargaining process began. Dad told me if I got a pass to one of those three schools, he would buy me a watch of my choice. Not to be outdone, Mum dangled the incentive of a bicycle.

There was a bit of a debate about whether I should have a bike, with my dad deeming it dangerous, which just made Mum dig her heels in. I remember being very excited about the possibility of a new watch and bicycle, but less so about studying. The exam was to be held in two parts, with the first at Welches Mixed school. While I was brushing my teeth in the bathroom on the morning of the exam, I recall Dad reminding me to cross all the t's and dot the i's. It was a tense few hours. You're never really sure with exams, are you? I thought I'd done alright, but it was still an anxious couple of weeks until I received news I'd passed the first part. The second part was held at Combermere, just outside Bridgetown, about five minutes from Barbados National Stadium. Again, I left home with messages of 'good luck' and timely reminders about the correct usage of commas, question marks, and full stops.

'You can only do your best,' said Mum, knowing the outcome might shape her son's future. She came with me on the bus from the village to Waterford and then walked across the Bow Road to Combermere, where the headmaster was waiting to welcome everyone. The tension was unbearable as the rules were read out. There would be three papers: English, Maths, and an essay about one of several given topics. When I'd finished and came out of the exam, Mum was waiting. I told her I thought I'd done alright in Maths and Essay but less so in the English paper. She asked what I'd written my essay on and was a little alarmed.

'My pet,' I replied.

'How could you?' she exclaimed, 'You haven't got a pet!'

'No, but I've got an imagination, Mum,' I said, thinking of this fantasy dog I owned.

During the following week, a major scandal broke in the newspapers, with revelations that some of the schools had received prior notification of the English paper in advance of the exam. A high-ranking Government official had leaked the paper. This meant everyone would have to re-sit the English part, giving me another opportunity to get that bit right. The next few weeks were even more tense, waiting for the results. Soon there was a rumour circulating that five children from Welches had passed and were eligible for the top four girl schools: Queen's College, St Michael's, Foundation

Girls and Alexandra, or the six elite boy schools: Harrison, Lodge, and Combermere, or the slightly less prestigious Foundation Boys, Coleridge & Parry, and Alleyne. One evening, just before the bell rang for the end of the day, everyone was called into the main hall, where the headmaster, Mr Edwards, announced that five pupils had been successful. Sherry-Ann Cummings and Carol Anne Sealy had received passes for Queen's College and St Michael's schools. There were shouts of delight from these two girls as those were the top two girls' schools. The next name read out was Mark Scott, who'd gotten into Alleyne. Then, 'Pedro Morris, Harrison College,' announced Mr Edwards. Now, I was worried. Only one more place, one more name to be read out. Everyone was hoping and praying, and the crying and laughter seemed to grow stronger. Finally, the headmaster begged for silence.

'The last full pass is Ricardo Husbands, Combermere School.'

My mind was scrambled with a thousand thoughts: bicycles, watches, the reaction of everyone at home! Most of all, I couldn't wait to tell Mum *My Pet* was the correct choice after all! Indeed, she was over the moon and promised to order the bike the very next day. Dad was still at work, so I had to wait a while before telling him the good news. He, too, was delighted. I felt both relief and pride as I went out to find my friends to play bat and ball with. A few were missing, presumably as punishment for not passing their exams. Mum and Dad honoured their promises. A lot of the other kids rode about on Raleigh Chopper bikes, but I wanted to be different and chose a brightly coloured purple '20' bike. I cherished that bike and the independence it gave me, allowing me to venture further away from the village and explore different areas of the island, usually wearing my new watch. Made by Fortis, it had a lovely big face, with big numbers and sweeping hands. I'd never felt so happy.

CHAPTER 3

RIDING WITH THE PM

The new academic term began in September 1975. Big school! My uniform was neatly ironed, my bag carefully packed, and my lunch box stocked with goodies. This was all a brand-new adventure, so mum accompanied me on the journey for my first day. Barring the understandable nerves, it was a fairly uneventful ride to Combermere, although there were a few road manners for me to learn. The Rocklyn Bus Company served that part of Barbados and operated open-sided buses. Mum was somewhat alarmed at this and told me never to sit at the end or put my head outside the windows.

Combermere seemed much bigger than when I'd visited for the exam several months earlier. There was so much noise as everyone tried to find their bearings and discover their classes, then we all had to meet the headmaster and the head boy (*head boy David Thompson went on to become the 6th Prime Minister of Barbados on 15 January 2008 but died in office on 23 October 2010).* to discover what was expected of us. When it was time for Mum to leave, she cried as she waved goodbye. It made me feel emotional, and I began to cry. Not a good start, but soon the tears were forgotten as I began to make new friends.

When classes were finished, I'd agreed to link up with Harry Bruce, my old friend from the village, who had earlier passed for Combermere. We decided that instead of catching the bus out of Bridgetown, we would catch one going into town and later get a bus home from the main terminal there. As we approached the main terminal, I noticed the boys didn't wait until the bus had stopped before hopping off. This looked like a cool thing to do, and when Harry did it, I decided to follow. The next thing I knew, I was rolling on the floor, battered and bruised. There was clearly an art to hopping off a bus! Hurt, embarrassed and lying on the ground, everyone gathered around me. Harry soon came to my aid, helping me back to my feet. A boy had been crushed under the bus a year earlier doing what I'd done. As you can imagine, all the way home, I dreaded having to tell Mum the reason for the cuts and bruises and my torn uniform. Her response was entirely predictable: 'You could have been killed!' Followed by a dreadful knocking; any hope of going out to play that evening was dashed!

It had been natural to tag onto Harry when first at Combermere, but as I became more independent, I'd go on my own and walk along the Bow Road, past the National Stadium. It is a 15-minute walk from there to school, but I figured I'd try and thumb a lift if the opportunity arose. One morning I did just that, and a massive, shiny car pulled up alongside. The first thing I spotted was its L plate (L was for vehicles registered in St Lucy, the northernmost parish on the island). It was a left-hand drive, so I nipped round the other side. There, I nearly jumped out of my skin.

'Get in boy,' the driver said.

It was the Prime Minister of Barbados! Errol Walton Barrow ('The Dipper') had led a full and interesting life, serving in the Royal Air Force during the Second World War, where he'd trained as a navigator, becoming highly decorated for his role in some of the most daring bombing raids. At the war's end, he was appointed personal navigator to the Commander in Chief of the British Zone of occupied Germany, Air Chief Marshall Sir William Sholto Douglas. He then turned his hand to politics, studying at the London School of Economics alongside other future political leaders: Forbes Burnham (Guyana), Michael Manley (Jamaica), Pierre Trudeau (Canada) and Lee Kwan Yew (Singapore). Barrow had become the leader of the Democratic Labour Party, and following independence from Great Britain in 1966, he became the first Prime Minister of Barbados.

Now, nine years later, he was talking to me! I thought, 'Shit, what do I do?' but opened the door anyway and sat beside him. 'Hello,' he said, 'How are you?' He then asked my name and explained he'd started his education at Combermere, before enquiring about the place nowadays. We were at the school gates all too soon, with the PM telling me to 'be careful' as I got out. As he drove away, I remember thinking, 'No-one will believe me,' and that's exactly how it was at school. 'Prime Minister, huh,' they sneered. It was a slightly different reaction at home, Mum telling me off for jumping in the car with a stranger. 'But he's not a stranger, Mum; he's the Prime Minister.' The incredible thing about this story is that it wasn't a one-off. Every now and again, as I was walking along the Bow Road,

I'd hear, 'Hey, Ricky, jump in,' as Mr Barrow pulled up alongside. Sometimes it would be once or twice a week; sometimes, the gap would be a little longer, but whenever he was on the way to his office and saw me, he'd give me a lift. This happened until he was voted out of office in September 1976. Our paths never crossed again, and he died in 1987.

I'm sure Mr Barrow would have enjoyed watching the US Navy fighter jets that frequently flew around the coastline. I can remember on several occasions taking my bike to the harbour, off the southwest corner of the island, to sit on the wall, watching the jets take off and land on the aircraft carriers that would moor just a little way out to sea. I was fascinated by the whole experience and couldn't imagine anything more exciting than being in the cockpit of one of those powerful machines as they roared away high into the skies. A tour of the carrier and my mind was made up. I can distinctly remember telling my dad about my ambition one day.

'Ricky, what are you going to do with your life?'

'I'd like to be a pilot, Dad.'

His answer will stay with me forever.

'Son, black people don't fly planes.'

Maybe he had never seen a black pilot, but surely it was possible, I thought as I walked away, slightly dejected. Looking back, I wish he'd still been alive when I became a pilot and flew into Bridgetown for the first time some 20 years later. I can imagine how proud he would've been. I'm sure there would have been a few glasses raised! Of course, that was all a long way in the future; back then, it looked like a cool thing to do, and I started to stick pictures of aeroplanes on our bedroom wall.

There were no further dramas or excitement that I can recall during my early terms at Combermere. However, I loved participating in sports and noticed the bigger boys playing cricket. So, I decided to try this more advanced game of bat and ball. Combermere has a massive reputation for producing cricketing talent. Some of the finest players to represent the West Indies have passed through its doors, including Sir Clyde Walcott, Sir Frank Worrell and Sir Wes Hall. The trend continues nowadays with recent internationals Carlos Brathwaite, Kraigg Brathwaite, Jomel Warrican, Roston Chase, Shane Dowrich, and England's Chris Jordan all having studied there.

Indeed, Brathwaite and Jordan were classmates with a certain Robyn Rihanna Fenty.

During a lunch break, I ran to the playing field and managed to get an early batting spot. First, I took my turn at fielding, and then, when it was my turn, I stepped forward to take the plywood bat. As I walked to the crease, an older boy stepped across me. 'I'll pay you 25 cents for your position,' he offered. I said no, but he took the bat anyway and with a slap, I was told to bowl the tennis ball instead. Bowling fast would be my only chance to gain revenge.

During the following year, I played more and more sports, soon representing the school at athletics. On my first sports day, I won gold medals in the high jump, long jump, 100 and 200 metres. All should have been good, but Mum and Dad weren't happy as they felt I was neglecting my studies. As a result, I was banned from playing sports for a while until a bare pass was good enough to move me to the next form. I would be outside at every opportunity, cramming my evenings with cricket practice, athletics training, and an occasional football match. The odd injury here and there was par for the course. One evening, during athletics training, I clipped a hurdle and went sprawling, tearing a ligament in my stomach. As we didn't have the funds for medical treatment, I went to see my grandmother for an 'old folks remedy', a concoction of candle grease, camphor, and some different leaves she picked from the gulley. It was all heated up and applied to the affected area.

I thought the foul smell alone would drive away the pain. Once again, I was reminded of the need to focus on my education and told that I couldn't play sports in the evenings. I began to rebel! If I couldn't play sport, I'd go to the cinema instead, which sometimes meant leaving school early. I joined in with a gang of youths who were always getting involved in fights and would hang around smoking. It was nothing too heavy, but I'd certainly become a problem child and refused to conform. I had my ears pierced and grew my hair into dreadlocks. The headmaster soon learned about our activities and sent letters to all the parents. Mum went to the school and had a heart-to-heart with him about my behaviour, but I was past caring by this stage. Inevitably, I failed my end-of-year exams and was made to spend another year in the second form. Dad was furious and wanted to give me a sound beating, but Mum stopped him and sought help from the church. She took me along every Sunday morning and made me attend Sunday school in the evenings. This was particularly hard for me, as I could see the other boys playing cricket on the journey there. At church, Reverend Knight pulled no punches: 'Shape up or you'll end up in Dodd's', he said. Dodd's was the local juvenile prison, carrying a terrifying reputation. I thought this was pretty extreme as I didn't think I was out of control, merely finding other ways to fill time because I wasn't allowed to play sports. I was missing cricket and explained this to Mum – again and again. As a last resort, and worried about how I was turning out, she allowed me to do sports again, presumably thinking I'd be too preoccupied to get into any more mischief. Success!

Soon all my time was taken up with cricket again. I was allowed to play in the evenings and every Sunday, with Mum even paying for me to join a local team. I hadn't had any proper coaching by this stage, and my skills were all fairly natural. Harold Brewster, who in his time had been the Barbados ambassador to England, was now retired and worked as a sports master at the school. He gave me lots of encouragement and tips but not a lot of coaching. He did pick me for the school under 15 side when I was just 12, playing alongside boys two years my senior, and I was playing first division cricket by the age of 14.

There was a caveat, though...The headmaster decreed that my schoolwork would have to improve, or I would be pulled out of the team. Determined to keep my part of the bargain, I worked hard over the next 12 months, both in and out of the classroom. Passing my next exams meant I could move up into the third year, prompting Mum and Dad to rekindle those conversations about their eldest son one day becoming a doctor. My career aspirations were very much up in the air, and I was beginning to wonder how far my cricketing skills could take me when I was given a boost by being chosen to participate in coaching sessions with some of the Kerry Packer World Series cricketers. World Series Cricket had been staged in Australia for a couple of years. It was brought to the Caribbean in early 1979 for some One Day Internationals and 'Super Tests' between West Indies and Australia. I was still only 13 at the time and was put into a group with Martin Kent, the Queensland and Australian batter. Every weekend and every evening was now tied up with cricket. Two boys in the village, Victor Sandiford and Ricky Harrison, played first division cricket and helped me with some of their second-hand kit. It was useful as I was now playing for the school on Saturdays and for the Welches team on Sundays. My schoolwork remained on track, and I graduated into the fourth form. I was now playing regularly for the Combined Schools side in the first division of the Barbados Cricket Association (BCA) league, competing against notable sides such as Carlton, Empire, Pickwick, Spartan and Wanderers. These sides were historically amongst the best on the island and had consistently provided cricketers to represent Barbados and the full West Indies side. Depending on their commitments, it wasn't unusual for us to be playing against some of the most famous names in the game, and a daunting experience to be bowling against the likes of Gordon Greenidge, Desmond Haynes or Collis King, all seasoned international players.

Batting wasn't any easier. In those days, we could expect to face bowlers of the calibre of Malcolm Marshall, Sylvester Clarke, Wayne Daniel and Ezra Moseley. It wasn't always fun, but you learnt quickly. One match stood out when we played against BCL, who had Clarke, Moseley and Franklyn Stephenson together in their attack. It was a big jump for us, but it gave schoolboys the experience of top-level cricket. Once I began to play matches regularly, I found that I could bowl really quickly and with a good rhythm. Onlookers would be quick to praise, but the best reaction was always seeing opposition batters being beaten for pace or ducking out of the way. Being so young did have its occasional drawbacks. In the Banks-sponsored Barbados first division, there was always a prize of two cases of Banks Beer to the man of the series. In one of my first appearances, I took 7-18 with the ball, won man of the series and was looking forward to collecting my award. Unfortunately (but sensibly!), they decided I was too young and gave me two cases of soft drinks instead.

Whilst cricket was very much my main focus, I was also starting to notice the opposite sex, and in particular, I noticed a beautiful girl who worked in the school canteen. Her name was Joyce, and I fancied her from the start. She gave me her telephone number, and I would ring her whenever possible. However, there was a problem; she was 23 and had a child. I was 15.

During the summer of 1980, I was selected by Combermere to play against an English touring side from Malvern College. The day before the match, I was having a bicycle race against some friends when I fell and took the skin off my chest, knees, elbows, and hands. Back home, this caused a furious row between my parents, with my dad insisting that I shouldn't have a bike. Knowing I'd got an important match the next day, I stayed out of the way and spent the evening cleaning and plastering my wounds.

However, despite my bumps and bruises, I could play; we won quite easily, I bowled quickly and picked up several wickets. Afterwards, three of the Malvern masters came over and introduced themselves. They were Geoff Morton, who had played for Middlesex, Andrew Murtagh, who'd played for Hampshire; and Alan Duff, a former Worcestershire player. They wondered if I'd ever thought about playing cricket in England. It all sounded a little fanciful to me. Finally, they explained that Malvern College was one of the most respected public schools in England, and it would be beneficial if I were to continue my education there. With a fee of £2,500 per term, it seemed a pipe dream.

CHAPTER 4
AN ENGLISH ADVENTURE

Several weeks after playing Malvern, I reflected on the opportunity. Realistically, I knew it would be impossible to raise the necessary funds but the masters hadn't forgotten about me, and I received letters from Alan Duff asking how I was and about my form on the cricket field. I would always send back my bowling figures from the matches I'd played. This went on until one day in December 1980. I was in class, and the head boy came and said that the headmaster wanted to see me. Had something happened to my brother or sister? Were Mum and Dad OK? My heart was racing as I neared the headmaster's office. He started by saying he'd received a letter from a college in England hoping to finalise a scholarship whereby I would be transferred there. Suddenly, panic turned to joy.

'This will have to be discussed with the school governing body,' he continued, 'And, of course, your parents!'

The rest of that day, I was in a daze. I couldn't wait to get home and tell my parents. They didn't share my excitement but Dad was more receptive to the idea than Mum. Meanwhile, the headmaster had put the wheels in motion. Soon, faxes were whizzing between him and Malvern, carrying information about the college and the people trying to organise the scholarship. Everyone seemed convinced it was a good idea. Everyone, that is, except Mum. I think she knew it was an excellent opportunity for me, but understandably she had reservations about me moving so far away. Those reservations were partly answered when Alan Duff gave her a call. He gave her all the assurances he could and even told her that it would be a trial; if things didn't work out, I would have the option of returning to Barbados and continuing my education at Combermere. Mum came off the phone and gave her blessing. I could go to England and continue my education there. I was overjoyed, and pretty soon, the whole village knew.

Despite Malvern taking care of my trip and all of the funding, the villagers knew I would need money for my expenses and everyday items, so they set about organising a series of fund-raising events, with dances, parties, and sponsored walks. Meanwhile, my performances on the cricket field were being noticed, and I was selected for Barbados under 19 trials. This was a big step for me, considering I was only 15. However, there was a problem. I was due to fly to England on 17 April 1981, and the under 19s tournament would be held in Guyana three days later. It wasn't possible to change the flight date, so I had to make a decision: represent my country or take up my place at Malvern. I sought the advice of those around me and the other boys in the village. The consensus seemed to be that time was on my side to play under 19s cricket, but I might never get another opportunity like Malvern had given me. With a little reluctance, I withdrew from the remainder of the trials.

My airline ticket was delivered to Barbados by the England touring team manager Alan Smith, whose son Mark would be a fellow pupil at Malvern. Even though I was only 15, he invited me to be a practice bowler and to attend the Test match. Watching my future Middlesex team-mate, Roland Butcher, become the first black player to represent England and Michael Holding bowl two of the fastest overs ever was a privilege although the Test was marred by the death of England coach Kenny Barrington from a heart attack at only 50 years old.

Mum wanted me around because there was so much to do before my flight. She'd kitted me out with new shoes, shirts and a couple of suits, but the biggest surprise of all was… a new name! Born out of wedlock, I'd taken my mum's maiden name, Husbands. But now my married parents decided both Dale and I should take their married surname. I was now Ricardo Ellcock.

The day before the flight was filled with phone calls from family and friends, all wishing me good luck. Lots of closer family members came around to see me, many of them bringing little gifts or pressing money into my hand for the journey. I remember the packing kept having to be re-done as a selection of socks, ties, and underwear continued to arrive at the house. On the Saturday, the day of my flight, I made a point of visiting everyone in the village to thank them. Down the road, at Pearl's rum shop, a full-on celebration was underway with plenty of pig foot, salt fish, and rum. The music coming out of the shop was deafening, and I remember Caleb, the deaf and dumb boy from the village, dancing around, having a great time. Mum was in a state, trying to attend to so many things, whilst obviously concerned her eldest son was about to fly off to a place she knew very little about and had never seen. I could hear her talking to friends, 'What if he can't handle the cold? What if he's mistreated by the people there? What if he doesn't like the flight? Suppose it crashes? What if there's no one to meet him at the airport?' So many things were going through her mind. Dad didn't appear to have any of those concerns, however. He had ordered a minibus to take everyone to the airport and plenty of rum for the journey. I went to get ready in the outside washroom. I returned to find Mum in tears; she was clearly struggling to deal with the situation.

The minibus arrived, already crowded. It was so full that Mum, Dale and Alison decided to go in another car with Cousin Norma. The bus was full of chatter and music, but I later learned it was a pretty sombre mood amongst those following in the car. A familiar face greeted us at the airport. 'Spoo', a one-eared man from the village, working as a sky cap (one of the porters who assisted with your luggage). He took my bags over to the Laker Airways counter to be checked in. That was the cue for all the men to head off to the bar, where dad delighted in telling everyone his son was going off to England to study. I stayed alongside Mum, comforting and reassuring her. I hadn't given much thought as to what lay ahead for me.

Before long, a crackle over the tannoy and a gentle lady's voice announced the first call for the Laker Airways flight to Luxembourg and Gatwick. Mum burst into tears, knowing it was time to say goodbye. Through her tears, she told me to behave myself, wear plenty of clothes, and call her as soon as I arrived. She was inconsolable as we parted. I kissed her, my sister, my cousins, and I shook hands with just about everyone at the airport before being handed to 'Ovey', a customs officer from the village. Without a look back, I walked through and onto the aeroplane. Ovey sat me in an aisle seat, shook my hand and wished me good luck. Now, I was all alone.

There would be time to reflect on what lay ahead over the next few hours, but for now, I tried to take in my new surroundings, the inside of a Laker Airways DC10 aircraft. Against a backdrop of a gentle buzz from the aircraft's systems, the cabin was filled with chatter and excitement as my fellow travellers blocked the aisles, looking for their seats and filling the overhead lockers. After what seemed an eternity, the doors were slammed shut, and the annoying buzz disappeared before suddenly becoming much louder. The lights dimmed and the plane began to shudder; peering across and out of the window, it appeared the plane next to ours was moving forward, but it couldn't have been as the terminal building was in front of us. We were reversing away smoothly before coming to a halt. My thoughts drifted towards Mum. I wondered how she was doing. Was this trip worth all the pain it had brought her? With another jerk, the aircraft was moving forward, slowly at first but then accelerating across the bumpy tarmac. 'Surely this wasn't fast enough to take off?' I thought before realising we were still taxiing towards the runway. One left turn, then another, and then the noise from the engine grew louder and louder. I thought back to those jets I'd watched so many times being catapulted into the skies as they took off from the aircraft carriers. I felt myself sinking into the seat as the aircraft accelerated; I looked across towards the cabin window to see the terminal building go flashing by. I braced myself as the nose rose, and I could feel my heart racing. There was a loud thud. I must have appeared concerned because a young girl sitting across the aisle looked at me and said, 'It's OK; it's the wheels being raised.' I told her it was my first time flying. My travel companion seemed nice, and we started to chat. She told me her name was Anna, and she was from Switzerland. She was a medical student in St Lucia. We chatted until I realised it was now dark outside.

A couple of familiar faces walked down the aisle and said hello. They were both local cricketers, and I'd seen them around cricket grounds from time to time and knew them as Alvin Greenidge, a future Test player, and Calvin Hope, who went on to become a high-ranking official within the Barbados Cricket Association. The two cricketers explained they were on their way to take up professional contracts in Holland.

A bell sounded over the PA system, then a voice said it was the captain speaking. He explained we were about to experience turbulence and that all passengers should remain seated with their seat belts fastened. I had no idea what this meant but started to panic as the ride became bumpy. Anna was once again on hand to explain this was perfectly normal. Eventually, tiredness took hold, and I fell asleep before being awakened by the captain announcing we had started our descent into Luxembourg. My ears were popping until Anna passed me a piece of chewing gum and told me to open my mouth as wide as I could and then start chewing. Next, I heard the wheels being lowered and looked out. It was misty, but I noticed the cars were driving on the wrong side of the road. Then, we were down, and I could feel the seatbelt straining as the brakes were applied before we gently taxied towards the airport. Moments later, the doors were opened; I wished Alvin and Calvin good luck as they departed.

I had been told it was a short stop in Luxembourg before the plane continued to Gatwick; Anna suggested there was still time for a short walk to the terminal building. Amongst my new clothes was a warm jacket; I popped it on and headed for the doorway. It was certainly needed! A blast of icy air was my first experience on European soil and a further reminder of how far I was from home. Everywhere I looked, I could see buggies overloaded with suitcases. Everything looked chaotic, and I felt the need to return to my seat. Soon we were on our way again and beginning our descent into Gatwick. I could see cars on the left-hand side of the road, the same as in Barbados. This time the landing was pretty bumpy, and a few passengers broke into applause as the crew wrestled the huge aircraft to the ground. The plane taxied to its allotted parking area, and everyone rose together, rummaging around in the overhead lockers. Anna leaned across and told me to follow her. At the bottom of the steps was a very long bus; she said we needed to board it for the journey to the terminal. Whilst waiting for it to be filled, I glanced back at our aeroplane and gasped at the sheer size of it. The whole place was huge. On this misty morning, it buzzed with life, with cars, vans, trucks, and planes all moving in a carefully coordinated rhythm. Anna clearly knew her way around and led me to the end of a very long queue, telling me I would need to show my passport when I got to the front. She would wait for me on the other side. Once I'd reached the front, a customs official examined my passport and looked at the detailed letter Alan Duff had sent me. With a friendly smile, he wished me a pleasant stay in England. Anna was waiting on the other side of the desk and escorted me to the baggage hall, which was even more crowded and confusing.

How could anyone ever find their bags? Soon, luggage started to arrive, and I spotted my suitcase. I struggled to get close enough to grab it before it disappeared through a little hole. I was panic-stricken, but Anna said it would be around again soon. It was time to say goodbye. She pointed me in the right direction and gave me a hug. I thanked her for everything and asked if we could keep in touch. We exchanged addresses, and she said goodbye.

All alone, I followed Anna's instructions, coming eventually to a glass door. There were many people waiting, some with sheets with names on but I couldn't see anyone I knew. Then I felt a tap on my shoulder. I looked around to see Alan Duff with a big smile on his face and an extra coat draped over his arm. He explained that the airport had told him the flight had been delayed, so he'd attended a Sunday morning service at the Gatwick chapel. I put the coat on as we walked to the car park, grateful for the extra protection against the biting wind. My bags were loaded into the back of Alan's green Renault estate, and we set off, carefully negotiating the twisty lanes of the car park. We soon came onto the biggest road I'd ever seen. Cars sped by, and when I looked, I could see Alan was doing 70mph (in Barbados, the limit is 30mph!)

Alan was keen to know how my family were and how the flight had been. 'You must be starving?' Before long, we turned off into a petrol station with a large restaurant. Roast beef Sunday lunch was ordered for us both. When it arrived, I asked about the bun. 'Yorkshire pudding,' said Alan. Back on the road, I saw a sign saying we were 35 miles from London. I knew we had many more miles to go, and the effects of a 10-hour flight meant it wasn't long before I drifted off. When I awoke, Alan said we were nearly there and pointed to a range of hills in the distance, 'The Malvern Hills. They stretch for 11 miles into Wales.' The hills grew larger as we neared them, and pretty soon we were driving alongside them. Then, some extraordinary buildings came into view. I thought it must be a church, but Alan said it was the main college block. 'Here we are; this is where we live.' One glimpse at the house had me thinking he must be very rich. A lady and two girls arrived at the door, and Alan introduced them as his wife, Sheila, and daughters, Claire and Susan.

'Come in; we'll get the bags later,' said Alan as I was whisked into the living room.

'Wow,' I thought, 'This one room is bigger than my whole house.'

Sheila asked who would like a drink, and I noted that Alan and Susan asked for tea with two sugars; Claire asked for tea with no sugar, so I asked for tea with one sugar to be on the safe side. There was a television set in the corner of the room with the pictures in colour. Suddenly, the channel changed. It startled me. I wondered how it had managed to do that on its own. I started to watch the new programme, and again, it changed! I looked around to see Susan (who had told me to call her Sue) with a little box in her hand. She said it was a remote control for changing channels. I was very impressed. Alan told me I ought to give my mother a ring and took me into another room. I dialled the number he gave me and after a few seconds, a lady answered.

'Can I speak to Marian Ellcock, please?'

'Ricky, Ricky, is that you?'

I had assumed I would have to speak to an operator before being put through but I recognised the unmistakable voice of my mum. She asked question after question, 'How are you?' 'How was the flight?' I told her everything, not forgetting the Yorkshire pudding and the magical remote control. Then I spoke to Dad, Dale, and Alison, who all sounded excited to hear from me. Mum said she loved me and told me to take care before asking to speak to Mr Duff. They chatted for a while before Alan rang off with lots of promises to look after me. The bags were fetched from the car, and I was taken to a room at the top of the building. There were three single beds, and I wondered how I would change my clothes if I shared with the two girls. Those fears were quickly dispelled.

'I'm sorry you will have to sleep alone on the first night, but the boys will be back tomorrow,' said Alan.

'Who are the boys?' I asked.

'School House is a boarding school, where 70 boys reside during term time,' explained Alan, 'There are ten houses in total, School House and houses one to nine. I'm the Housemaster of School House. The other boys will be returning from their Easter holidays tomorrow.'

Alan told me Mr Clarke would be over to meet me tomorrow. Mr Clarke, I learned, was the Birmingham businessman who had agreed to pay my school fees and plane ticket across to England.

'After you put your clothes away, come down for supper,' said Alan, leaving me to acquaint myself with my new surroundings. Looking out of the window, I could see the main college building to the left; over a steep bank, I spotted a lush green field. The evening sun reflected a pattern on it, like a draughts board. I thought it was so clever to create something like that and wondered how long it took. Then, in the distance, a horn sounded, and moments later, a train came into view. It was the first time I'd seen a train other than on television or in a picture. I unpacked my bags, put my clothes in the ample drawers and cupboards, and got changed out of my smart suit. It was so cold, so I put on as many layers of clothing as possible before returning downstairs and sitting in front of the television. The others were in the kitchen, so I thought I would try the magical remote control. I pressed a button, and the screen went blank. 'Oh no, I've broken it,' I thought and stumbled out an apology to Alan, who laughed and explained I'd only switched it off.

Over supper with the family, everyone seemed interested in hearing about my life in Barbados, and soon it was time to go upstairs. It had been a very long day, but in bed I wrote letters to Mum, Joyce, and Anna. I lay there thinking about what they'd all be doing. Dad would probably be at Pearl's shop, Dale playing down the street, and Alison round at Haa's house. And Mum? I knew she would be so worried about me and probably trying to take her mind off things by cooking. Before long, I was asleep. My English adventure had begun.

CHAPTER 5

JAM AND MARMALADE

I awoke refreshed after my first night's sleep in England and was already dressed by the time Alan looked in. He pointed towards the field I had noticed the previous evening. 'That, over there,' he explained, 'Is the first XI cricket ground.' I'd never seen such a well-groomed ground and couldn't wait to play on it. After breakfast, I was in the sitting room; the television on. This was surprising, as programmes in Barbados didn't start until 5pm. I heard the doorbell ring and could make out Alan welcoming someone. Moments later a gentleman and lady entered. I stood up and said hello; Alan then introduced Mr Michael Clarke and his girlfriend, Sandy. They sat, and we talked about Barbados; it was evident Mr Clarke had been several times and was very familiar with the island and its geography as he asked about the Coral Reef Hotel. He also wondered if the beaches were still the same or if the coast had been turned into a 'concrete jungle' with tourist hotels. 'The last time we were there, we did some island hopping but felt Bajans were the most hospitable,' said Sandy. She mentioned a couple of anxious moments whilst flying between the islands with LIAT. Mr Clark said he owned several office equipment stationers and printing businesses around England and that Sandy was a police markswoman in Birmingham. She was a very beautiful redhead and, I guessed, a lot younger. They both seemed very interested in everything I had to say and promised to come back and see me often. Mr Clarke mentioned he had opened an account with Mr Hunt, the local fruit and cake shop that had served him when he was at Malvern as a schoolboy. If I wanted anything else, I was to tell Mr Duff.

When they had gone, Alan took me down to the school shop to be kitted out in my school uniform. There, I met Geoff Morton, who managed the shop and coached the boys. Geoff asked me about my parents and then handed over my school uniform, which consisted of a plaid blazer, two plain blue shirts, a grey jumper, two pairs of grey trousers, and a pair of black shoes. The clothes were clearly second-hand, very much a case of 'let's see if these will fit'. The trousers were short in the leg and big in the waist, the jacket sleeves were too short and the jumper sleeves too long. Geoff mentioned there was a cricket match the coming Saturday, so I would need equipment as well, and he supplied a short and long-sleeved jumper. It was the first time I'd ever owned any jumpers.

Back at the house, the boys had started arriving for the new term, and I could hear the clatter of footsteps up and down the stairs. It seemed as if the kitchen had also stirred into action with lots of pots and pans banging. Up in the room were two other lads, and Alan introduced them as Gary Lea and Tom Orchard. Gary said he was South African but lived in Zambia and was a keen swimmer. His uncle was also a tutor at the college. Tom was the son of a Worcestershire farmer and had an older brother in the house. When Gary and Tom finished unpacking, they offered to show me around the house, pointing out the dining room before going down the stairs to the games room. I saw what I thought was a pool table, but most of the balls were red and had no numbers. Back out of the games room, Gary pointed to the noticeboard and explained all house news would be posted there. Through the door and to the left was the kitchen and out of bounds. Along the corridor was the television room; they explained the channel to be watched was decided by a vote of everyone in the room at the time. Across the corridor was the laundry room, where dirty clothes were to be dropped off in named bags on Fridays and picked up on Thursdays. All clothes had to be named with tags from Matron. To the left, Gary knocked on a door, and a slim man with thinning hair opened it. Gary introduced him as Mr Frayne, a house tutor but also Gary's uncle.

'If you have a problem you don't want to discuss with the housemaster, I'm always here to help,' he offered. We then continued our tour of the grounds and buildings. In the centre of the courtyard was an impressive statue of St. George, and I was told the grass verges around it were strictly out of bounds. I had no idea who St. George was, and my eyes were equally drawn to the two cement creatures flanking him. 'They're gryphons,' explained Tom as we hurried on. I was none the wiser. Were they real animals? Were they something I was likely to encounter here in rural Worcestershire?

There were three doors, one straight ahead of us for masters and prefects and one each to the left and right for general use. We went

44

through the door on the right, and my two guides showed me where the drinks machine was and then led me along a long corridor. All along the corridor were classrooms, and Gary explained each master had his own classroom and students moved between classrooms. This was the opposite of how it was done at Combermere. Further along the corridor, Gary pointed out the staffroom. Just then, a gentleman dressed in green came into view. When he had passed, Gary said, 'He has a register of every lesson and classroom, so if you are ever lost, go and see him.' Up the stairs, Gary said, 'This is Grundy.' It was a library. Along the corridor were the language rooms. Back down the stairs and through the doors was the chapel. Tom said, 'Everyone has to go to chapel on Mondays, Wednesdays, Thursdays and Sundays.' Across the road from the chapel were the main library and the science labs. Beyond them were the tennis courts, and down the hill were the racquets courts, fives courts and theatre. Across from the theatre was the cricket ground, and further down the hill was the driving range and a second cricket ground. Next to the cricket ground was the woodwork room, weights room, swimming pool, and indoor sports centre. My head was starting to spin now from so many places!

Further down the hill, as far as the eye could see, were football and rugby pitches. Then they pointed out Hunt's fruit and cake shop. All the way back to the house, Gary kept pointing out other houses, squash courts, art blocks, the school hospital, the music block and finally back to schoolhouse's own playing area. I couldn't understand why the boys did any work when there was so much else to do.

When we'd finished our tour of the school and the grounds, Gary showed me to the study we would be sharing with another lad, Andrew McCormick. Andrew was there, listening to a 'ghetto blaster'.

'Hi,' he said, 'Do you like The Jam?'

'What kind?' I queried.

'Not the kind you eat,' he laughed, 'The band!'

I'd never heard of them but thought I'd better say yes. Suddenly, a bell started ringing loudly.

'Come on,' said Gary. 'It's supper time.'

In the dining room, a queue of boys moved slowly towards a serving hatch, where Gary introduced me to Matron. I was handed a plate of mashed potatoes, sausage, and onion gravy. 'This is called bangers and mash,' said Gary as I examined the food. After quickly polishing it off, we returned to the hatch window, and each took a bowl containing a sponge with a yellow sauce. 'And this is spotted dick and custard.' The names meant very little, but it all tasted good, so I didn't mind what it was called!

Afterwards, Mr Duff came in and welcomed all the new boys. There were a few notices to hand out and a cautionary word asking everyone to work hard throughout the term. Back in the study, the music was again deafening, and Gary shouted above it to tell me where to put all my books after I'd collected them tomorrow. The bell rang again, and it was time for the ghetto blaster to be turned off. I sat back, not knowing what I'd made of 'The Hustle' or any of the tunes Andrew had tried to interest me in. After Gary announced it was bedtime, we went upstairs to find the washing area congested with boys brushing their teeth. Tom was already in bed when we returned, and I was putting my pyjamas on when the door burst open, and Andrew rushed in, playing an imaginary guitar and singing, 'Wish I could be like David Watts'.

I had no idea who David Watts was but guessed that was one of the many things I'd understand as my time at Malvern went on. When Andrew finished singing, he came and sat on my bed. Tall and slender, he told me he came from Sheffield in Yorkshire. A cheeky sort of lad, I liked him immediately. For his part, he wanted to know all about my life and what Barbados was really like. He wanted to know how good I was at cricket and if I'd played against Viv Richards. Before I could answer, Mr Duff entered the room and tapped his watch. Andrew nervously said, 'Sorry, I was just leaving,' and hurried out of the door. The housemaster then pointed out it was now 10.15pm and lights out should have been at 10pm. With that, he said goodnight and turned the lights off.

I couldn't sleep; it had been such a whirlwind of a day. How I wished Combermere had all the facilities here at Malvern. My mind was scrambled about what lay ahead. Would I be able to do all the schoolwork? The other nagging worry was whether I would be treated differently by the other boys, as I had seen no other black person.

At some point, I drifted off to sleep, but all too quickly a boy pushed the door open, ringing a bell. It was morning. Gary was first up and told me the morning bell ringing was a job everyone had to take turns doing. Getting ready, I saw a line of people waiting to use the bathroom, and I couldn't get to the shower. Gary explained that many boys chose to have a shower in the afternoon. This seemed strange, but I wasn't about to argue, so I quickly dressed and followed Gary to the dining room. The breakfast queue moved quicker than the previous evening, and when I got to the front, I chose the scrambled eggs and some crispy bacon. On the dining room tables were saucers and teacups laid out, plus a mountain of sliced bread. Gary pointed out that laying the tables was another task I would have to do in the future. Next to the windows stood some very weird-looking machines. Gary got up, grabbed a few slices of bread and moved over to the machines. He returned to the table with burnt bread and proceeded to plaster it with butter and then a very thick jam. Gary informed me it was 'marmalade.' He was enjoying it so much that I thought I'd try some. It didn't taste too bad! I was informed we weren't allowed back into the dormitories after breakfast, so we headed to the study, where we found the ghetto blaster blaring out and Andrew singing 'Baggy Trousers' at the top of his voice. Mr Duff's arrival signified it being switched off immediately, and I sensed this was a recurring issue between them. Andrew apologised and promised to keep it turned down a little, with Mr Duff stating it would be the best course of action or 'the stereo would be confiscated for a while'. Turning to me, he said, 'Work hard and enjoy it.' I followed Gary out of the door; he seemed to run everywhere. A pile of books was waiting at the bookshop, and all I had to do was choose some pens. I was told having a good fountain pen was important because all exams had to be written in real ink.

All sorted, then it was off to the first lesson of the day, English with Mr Murtagh, whom I'd met in Barbados the previous August. He asked me about the flight, my family, and how I was settling in. I don't think I heard much of the lesson, as I spent most of the time looking around and making comparisons. Gone were the shared desks and the chalkboards of Combermere. Things were more isolated here: one desk, one pupil. How different everything seemed. Gone were the short khaki trousers, khaki shirts and long blue and gold socks. Instead, everyone wore long trousers, ties, and jackets.

Looking around, I saw a boy pulling a strange face; I smiled as Andrew reached forward to call him a poof. Gary must have noticed as he leaned towards me from the next desk and said, 'Pay attention.' Mr Murtagh was speaking, and most of the other boys were taking notes, so I thought I ought to do the same and got my pen and pad out. It was all very difficult to follow. My mind wandered towards lunchtime, and I wondered if some of the boys would be going to the fields to play cricket. Suddenly I was startled as a buzzer went off. Mr Murtagh stopped talking, and everyone began packing their things away. 'Come on,' said Gary. And off we went, out of the door and up the stairs into another classroom. 'It's history now.' The teacher hadn't yet arrived, so I told Gary I hadn't understood much about the English lesson. 'Don't worry,' he replied, 'You can copy my notes later.'

Mr Turner was the history master, grey-haired, and at least 70 years old. I was determined to follow this lesson and take notes, but I was quickly out of my depth. I'd been learning about the Arawaks and the cannibalistic Caribs, whereas Mr Turner's lesson was on the Tudors and Stuarts. I had no idea about these people but tried to write everything down, hoping to make sense of it later. 'Just do the important bits,' whispered Gary, noticing I'd already filled two sides of paper. I had no idea what was important and what wasn't. After the lesson, Mr Turner asked me to stay behind for a moment and said he'd be happy to give me some extra lessons to help catch up.

Thankfully, it was time for lunch, so we headed back to School House. The tables were laid out with steel pans full of food. It was very noisy, with boys banging their knives and forks on the tables. A boy was holding a bell at the door leading from the private side; when he rang it, the noise stopped immediately, and everyone stood up. Through the door walked the masters. Mr Duff sat on the top table, and the others at various other tables. Finally, someone boomed, 'For what we are about to receive, Lord, make us truly thankful.' Everyone then sat down and started to help themselves from the steel pans. The meal consisted of boiled potatoes, cabbage, meatballs, and gravy.

After the main course, one person from each table moved to the window and collected the next course: apple pie and custard. When everyone had finished, the head table stood up. It was the cue for most of the masters to leave. When they had gone, Mr Duff read out notices before asking a few boys to meet him in his study, an instruction that provoked laughter throughout the dining room. Mr Duff walked out, and the boys whose names he had called followed. I was then confronted by a very stern-looking woman – Matron! She instructed me to follow her to the dormitory, where she explained that I needed to make my bed before going downstairs each morning. I hadn't been told, so I had to do it with this lady standing over me. There was only one thick blanket on each bed, so it didn't take long, and Matron seemed content. She told me to bring the duvet cover and pillowcases down for washing on Fridays, along with the rest of the dirty washing. I was also given some name tags to put in all my clothes. I returned to a very noisy study and wondered when everyone would go to the playing fields. I asked Gary, 'When do we play sports?' He explained that during the summer, games were played after classes.

Time for more lessons, and then back to the house for afternoon tea, scones and jam before everyone changed into their whites and moved to the cricket fields.

In the corner of the field were more nets than I'd ever seen, and boys were coming from all directions with their cricket equipment. At the back of the nets, I spotted Geoff coming from the shop with his walking stick. Down the hill came Mr Murtagh and Mr Duff. I recognised a few of the boys from the match in Barbados, and one or two of them came over to say hello.

Geoff hugged me before saying to take it easy because it was very cold and it would be easy to pull a muscle. Taking his advice, I eased myself into the session and found a good rhythm and pace. I was delighted with how it had gone because it had been several weeks since I'd last bowled. It had been a good first session, and I was thoroughly ready for the nice hot shower awaiting me on our return to the house. We were dressed in time for the supper bell and polished off a plate of boiled rice and chicken curry sauce.

Everything at Malvern seemed to be strictly controlled by the clock. Gary told me we would have two hours of Hall from 7.30pm after supper. I asked what Hall was and received two different answers. Andrew piped up with, 'It's two hours in your study listening to music,' whilst Gray corrected him, 'No, it's two hours in your study doing homework or reading!' A bell rang to signify it was 7.30pm, and everything fell quiet, except for a boy fixing his desk and chair at the bottom of the corridor. Andrew said, 'He is the guard; if you want to leave your study, he has to give permission.' You could hear a pin drop when he had finished fixing his desk and chair. I began copying Gary's notes from the English lesson whilst Andrew put on his Jam record. Occasionally, Gary whispered, 'Turn it down.' He did, but minutes later, he turned it up again. Slowly, the door opened, and Andrew quickly turned his machine off. It was the boy from the bottom of the corridor, hissing, 'I can hear that music from down the corridor.' Andrew promised to play it lower, but as soon as the prefect walked out of the door, the volume was turned up again. After I'd copied Gary's English notes, he gave me a history book to read. Andrew opened a packet of biscuits and was boiling his kettle when the door slowly opened, and Mr Duff walked in. Andrew was told his music was too loud and was disturbing everyone in the other studies. 'It's the first day, and you've already been told to turn it down three times,' said Mr Duff, 'If this continues, I will have to take the machine away.' Turning to me, he said, 'How was your first day, Ricardo?'

'It was OK,' I replied.

Mr Duff walked out of the door, and Andrew broke into an impersonation of him, ending it with a chuckle and a puff on an imaginary pipe. At 9.30pm, the bell rang, signifying the end of Hall. Again, the doors started slamming, and the boys ran around. Gary had to go and lay the tables for breakfast, so I climbed the stairs, brushed my teeth and changed into my pyjamas.

Nets had been fun, and several boys came in and asked me about my cricket. They wanted to know how fast I could bowl, had I ever hit anyone. They were also keen to know about Barbados and what it was like. However, I had some questions of my own.

'When can we watch television?'

I was told the older boys could watch television between 9.30 and 10pm during the week, and all boys could watch at weekends until 10pm. Younger boys were not allowed to watch at all during the week. A prefect opened the door, asked everyone to go to their rooms, and turned the lights off.

Questions inside still burned. I couldn't understand why the lights had to go out at 10pm and why I couldn't watch television during the week. Why was there a door only for prefects and masters, and how did the boys decide which sport to play? As my thoughts turned to Barbados, I remembered I hadn't posted my letters. It would get dark back home, and the boys would have stopped playing in the streets. Mum would have finished cooking, and Dale and Alison would probably be eating before being allowed to watch television until they fell asleep. Dad would have stopped by Pearl's shop for a drink with the other men in the village. All these thoughts made me sad that I wasn't there. I was overcome with emotion now and began to cry. This new life wasn't for me, I decided.

I was homesick, and it was probably best I returned to Barbados.

CHAPTER 6

INTO THE ROUTINE

A new morning brought a different mindset. Was I prepared to give up on this opportunity so easily? A lot of people had put themselves out to give me a chance of making something with my life. I owed it to them to at least try.

Up early, I washed my face, brushed my teeth and took my place in the breakfast queue. After setting myself up for the day with toast and marmalade, I packed my books for the morning and filled my new pen with ink. The afternoon classes went well, and I didn't feel out of my depth; by tea time, I was looking forward to the evening net session. Andrew had other ideas.

'I'm going uptown to the café for a fag,' he whispered.

'What's a fag?' I queried.

'A smoke, you know, a cigarette?'

Naively, I asked if that was allowed. I left him to it, got ready for nets, and was pleasantly surprised to see how many other boys were there. I felt good, so I increased my speed a little and struck the opening batter, Richard Bache, on the arm. He was clearly in some discomfort, and the masters halted the session there and then. Back at School House, it seemed as if the news had spread quickly. After supper, it was back to the study for Hall time. Two hours of studying was a new experience; normally, I'd wanted to get my homework over as quickly as possible. However, Hall was made more bearable with access to plenty of coffee and biscuits.

Afterwards, several of the boys came and wanted to ask more questions. Was I bowling at full pace yet? Didn't I like Richard? Was that my full run-up? Our chat was interrupted by the slow opening of the door and the familiar sight of Mr Duff. Most of the other boys quickly made their excuses and left as Mr Duff asked me how my schoolwork was going. 'I think all the subjects, except history, are going OK,' I told him. Mr Duff explained that the history master had recognised this and would be giving me extra lessons.

I thought about my new schoolmates as I lay in bed that night. All the boys seemed so contented and happy. Did they ever think of home? I wondered how they could spend so much of their lives away from their parents and doing so much work.

The usual morning routine was briefly broken in the dining room when Mr Duff walked in with a bag of mail, a treat that included three letters for me. I recognised the first one as being from Mum and the other two from Joyce and Anna. This reminded me I'd still not posted my letters yet. I ran to the study to get them and then asked Mr Duff to post them. In her letter, Mum said how much she was missing me and wanted to know what the weather was like, Joyce hoped I'd not met any girls, and Anna wondered what Malvern was like and if I'd got there safely. Gary came bursting through the door to say we were late, explaining that Thursday morning's school assembly was held in the main chapel. I grabbed my tie, blazer, and books and followed him outside, where I saw a stream of boys coming up the footpaths. In the chapel, Gary led me to the School House section, and I noticed all the masters were sitting at the back facing their classes.

'It's so they can see who misses assembly,' muttered Andrew.

I thought this was more like a church service than a school assembly, as we sang hymns and listened to readings from the Bible. It was certainly nothing like we used to have at Combermere. It was the first time I'd seen the whole school in one place, and as I looked up and down the rows in front of me, there was one thing I couldn't help but notice.

Apart from me, there wasn't a single black person there.

I looked down the rows to the left. None. The rows to the right. None. Finally, turning towards the back, I noticed a boy of mixed race who spotted me and smiled in my direction. But no one else was black, so I suddenly became very conscious of my skin colour. It felt like I stood out from everyone else; they were all looking at me. Suddenly, I could feel myself blush and wish I wasn't there. I ran straight to class when chapel ended, feeling very embarrassed. Gary arrived late, having been back to the house looking for me. I apologised to him at lunch before he explained there were no classes on Thursday afternoon. 'During summer, everyone goes into town for a walk on the hills before games,' he said. So, I walked with him and Andrew as we made the short journey, the first time I'd been away from the school grounds.

The town was bustling, and I observed a lot of girls around, dressed in various school uniforms. Andrew followed my gaze, 'All the girls in purple are from Malvern Girls, the ones in grey are Lawnside, the ones in brown are Ellerslie, and the ones in blue and yellow are from the Chase.' He added, 'But don't bother with the girls from the Chase because they are all scrubbers.' I wondered what a scrubber was but didn't ask. The girls from Ellerslie wore the same uniform as the school by the same name in Barbados, so I wondered if there was a link. Then, a couple of boys screeched around a corner in a BMW. Gary shouted, 'Show-offs!' and said they were Arabs from the Abbey International School. Andrew suggested I join him for a fag up on the Malvern Hills, but I turned him down and went with Gary to get a coffee at the Abbey Hotel instead.

Back at the house, in the 'Apathy room', several boys were reading the newspapers. The papers were a different texture from those in Barbados. I read the report from Antigua, where England was about to lose the fifth Test to the West Indies and the series 5-0. Again, the questions started from some of the other boys. Could I bowl as fast as Michael Holding? Would I play for the West Indies? It seemed like many of the boys were genuinely interested, and I answered as many of them as I could before leaving to get dressed for practice.

On the first XI ground, the stumps were up in the middle. Mr Murtagh came over to say the practice session would be held in the middle. The umpires were Mr Murtagh and Mr Morton, who sat on his shooting stick throughout. It gave me an opportunity to have my first bat in English conditions, and it turned into a nightmare. The ball was so slow that I kept playing shots too early and was finally caught for very little. However, I had a very good bowl and noticed the ball swung a lot more than it did in Barbados. Friday morning provided the worst weather I'd seen so far; it was raining and very cold. After only doing a half day of lessons the day before, Fridays seemed to go on forever, and then they announced it was too wet for outdoor nets, so we had to be indoors. Assuming the weather would improve, I was ready to start playing competitive cricket. On the noticeboard was an announcement about a match the following day, between pupils and masters. I was pleased to see I had been selected, so after Hall, I collected my cricket kit from the lockers and took it up to the dormitory, where I gave my bat and boots a good clean. Some of the boys gathered around, as they'd never seen anyone do that before.

The lights soon went out for bed. I couldn't sleep. All I could think about was tomorrow's match.

Waking early, I rushed to the window and saw it had stopped raining, but it looked extremely cold outside. I took my cricket gear down to breakfast, which produced a few laughs. After breakfast, on the way to the lockers, Tom was in the hallway and mentioned Gary had been looking for me. 'Why?' I asked. 'Because you will be late for lessons,' he responded. I had no idea there were lessons on Saturdays. Returning to the study, I dressed in record time and ran to the first lesson. I just about made it. I could tell Gary had been panicking and was relieved to see me. 'What about the cricket?' I wanted to know. 'When will the game be played?' Gary told me Saturdays were half-day lessons, but cricketers were allowed to leave early for games. It didn't matter for today's game because it was scheduled to begin at 1.30pm.

The morning dragged, but eventually, it was time to play. I got changed in the drying cupboard and spent the duration of our innings looking through the dressing room window. Then, just before the innings were about to close, I noticed what appeared to be pebbles falling from the sky. In a matter of seconds, the ground was completely covered. It looked amazing but brought a halt to the match, so I walked onto the outfield and picked up a handful – they were like ice cubes. The captain of our team, Mark Woof, must have noticed my reaction. 'Hailstones,' he said. It wasn't long before the match was called off.

I noticed some of the masters keeping warm with a glass of whisky while we went to the house to get warm with a cup of coffee.

It hadn't been the day I had hoped for, and it was disappointing not to get a bowl. Instead, Gary and I decided to relax in the television room and watch sports until supper. He left at the sound of the bell, but I was enjoying it so much that I thought I'd give supper a miss for once. A little while later, another bell rang, but I thought someone must be playing around with the bell. Being the only one in the television room, I was enjoying the luxury of choosing which channel I wanted to watch. It was a rarity to have some me time, but then the door burst open.

'Why are you here?' demanded Matron.

I told her I was watching the television. She told me Hall had already started and I should get there now. I ran out quickly, not knowing there was also Hall on Saturdays. Gary then reiterated the rules, 'You are only allowed to watch television on Saturdays after sport and before supper and then after Hall until 10pm.' Ridiculous, I thought! I decided once again I'd had enough of life at Malvern and couldn't handle the strictness any longer. There were too many rules, it was always cold, and you did nothing but work and sleep. If I were back in Barbados, at least it would be warm, I could play out in the evening until whatever time I wanted and go to sleep when I felt like it. When the bell rang to signify the end of Hall, all the other boys rushed to the television room to get in their half-hour, but I went straight to bed. I'd had enough. I was going to phone Mum and ask her if I could come home.

I must have cried myself to sleep, and when I awoke, there was lots of excitement. 'It's snowing,' exclaimed Andrew. Outside, everything was completely white. Dressing quickly, I ran downstairs. It appeared different to what I'd seen on television and postcards. I wondered what it felt like, but my first experience wasn't positive because a snowball struck me on the head as I walked out of the door. And it hurt!

I retreated indoors and dressed for chapel. The short distance there seemed to last forever, and by the time I arrived, I could no longer feel my fingers or toes. When chapel finally finished, the other boys hung around and had snowball fights, but I ran back and dressed in every sock and jumper I could find. Feeling low, I sought out Mr Duff and asked if I could phone Mum. He dialled the number, and I waited for it to be answered. I burst into tears as soon as I heard her voice.

'Whatever is the matter, Ricky?'

'It's snowing, it's too cold, you're not allowed to watch television, and you must be in bed by 10pm.'

'Oh Ricky, you've got to stick it out and try your best,' she said and gave the phone to Dad.

He sounded stern, 'This is the best chance you'll ever get, Ricky, and you've got to stick it out.'

I said I'd give it some more time, and it was agreed that if I still felt the same way at the end of term, I'd return to Barbados. Mr Duff saw how upset I was and offered me some words of comfort. Then he called Gary and asked him to take photos of me in the snow to send to Mum. Cheered up, I agreed, went outside and quite enjoyed the snowball fights.

In the afternoon, Mr Duff again called me to his study and explained that all boys find the first weeks at boarding school hard. He knew I was looking forward to the cricket and said, 'As the summer gets hotter, there will be many more things to do.' He also said I could spend the summer holidays in England or return to Barbados. That night I went to bed feeling better and more determined to be a success.

My first match for Malvern was against Dean Close school in Cheltenham. I had been told to go to lessons that Saturday wearing my whites, blazer and tie. It felt silly to be dressed like that, especially with black school shoes. Nevertheless, I was excited to be playing and relieved when it was time to leave lessons.

The trip there seemed to last for ages; I couldn't visualise a journey of that length anywhere in Barbados. We arrived at our destination and elected to field first after winning the toss. The wicket was extremely slow, and I bowled much too short for the conditions but still ended up with a couple of cheap wickets. The rain began to fall at the start of our innings, and the match was abruptly called off. I found it all very disappointing for the second week in a row. Did they ever manage to complete a cricket match in England? Is it always this cold?

Does it rain every Saturday?

Many other unanswered questions were running through my head as I pondered the day's play. The wicket had been very slow, and I was concerned they might all be like that. Mr Duff passed on a lot of tips over the next few days, and as the weather improved, the wickets got harder, and I could bowl a little faster and score a few runs. It was clear by then the word was getting out about my performances, and the other schools were becoming wary of Malvern's young West Indian fast bowler. One or two of them even objected to me playing! Indeed, at most school games, there was real hostility from opposing masters and kids. One of the attractive fixtures we had lined up was against Worcestershire's second XI. I was particularly looking forward to this as I expected it to be a real challenge against a county side. As I made my way to the cricket field, I passed several cars with the names of players and their sponsors on the side. The Worcestershire players had already arrived and were practising on the outfield. I was a little surprised, however. They just looked like any other team. I half expected them to be wearing pretty hats and tracksuits; instead, they wore whites and boots just the same as I did.

Malvern lost the toss, and Worcestershire elected to bat first. As I marked out my run, I looked up to the pavilion and noticed the batters were wearing helmets. My hands were shaking as the umpire called 'Play', and I crossed myself and said a little prayer. I set off, but as I got closer, I could feel myself getting more and more nervous. I decided to stop. I walked slowly back to my mark and ran in again, accelerating naturally and releasing the ball at the optimum moment. The batter played and missed; it thudded into the wicket-keeper's gloves. There was a smile on my face as I walked back; that one delivery had given me all the confidence I needed. By the end of the Worcestershire innings, I'd picked up four wickets and had hit my future friend Damian D'Oliveira on the helmet.

News of that incident was soon all over the school and then around the other schools. I returned to my room that night feeling very pleased with myself and wrote to everyone I could think of to tell them about the match. But unfortunately, my head was full of the day's events, and it got me into trouble the next day at school when Mr Walwyn, the Physics teacher, asked me a question. Dreaming of glories, I hadn't been listening.

The master looked sternly at me, 'If you don't listen to what I'm saying, I will ask you to leave.'

He left it at that.

Soon, however, my thoughts drifted again towards cricket. It really wasn't my day because I felt the glare of anticipation again, the angry Walwyn staring me down for another interrogation.

'I'm waiting, boy!'

Failing to answer, I was asked to leave the lesson, with the words, 'And don't come back until you learn to pay attention,' following me out the door. Close to tears, I slowly returned to School House, fearing the outcome. What a difference 24 hours had made! It wasn't a great surprise when I was told during lunch Mr Duff wanted to see me in his study. The other boys laughed and came up with all sorts of punishments I would likely get.

Telling the truth seemed to be the only defence I could offer, so I told Mr Duff I hadn't been fully concentrating during the Physics lesson and that my mind had been on the cricket match. Of course, any of the other masters might not have been so forgiving, but Mr Duff knew how much cricket meant to me, although he warned me it must not get in the way of my schoolwork, or he'd stop me playing.

As I returned to the study, I vowed never again.

On 17 June, I was awakened by the sound of the door squeaking gently open and Mr Duff standing there, holding a cup of tea and some biscuits with chocolate on the top. 'Happy birthday, Ricardo,' he beamed as he handed me the tea and biscuits. He told me that once I was dressed, I could ring home. Tom peeped out from under his duvet, and Gary sat up in bed and explained everyone gets tea and chocolate hobnobs as a treat on their birthday. I'd never heard the word hobnobs before and asked why they were called that. My roommates weren't much help; 'That's just what they're called,' answered Tom, leaping out of bed. 'Don't you have them in Barbados?'

Later, Mr Duff called for me and announced he had my mum on the phone. I followed him to his office and sat beside the phone as he left the room. Mum wanted to know everything I'd been doing and all about the weather and if I was warm enough. I didn't like my trousers and told her I needed some new, warmer ones, so she asked me to send her a piece of material so she could match them. I told dad about the Worcestershire second XI match and then spoke to Alison, Dale, and Haa. It was lovely to hear from them all, and I would have talked all day had Mr Duff not returned and said he thought I should end the call, as it would be costing my family a lot of money. Mum said everyone in the village was asking about me, so I asked her to say hello to them all before saying goodbye.

Hearing everyone's voices had been a great start to the day, and I rushed back to the study and cut a piece of material from the fold of my trousers for mum before returning to give the letter to Mr Duff. I was now feeling settled at Malvern and knew it wouldn't be too long before it was July and time to go home for the summer holidays. At least that was the plan – and you know what they say about plans!

On the first day of July, after lunch, Mr Duff read the notices and asked to see me in his study. The whole house erupted in laughter, as this usually meant the pupil was in trouble. I looked quizzically towards Gary. I knew I'd done nothing wrong, but he just shrugged his shoulders. Fearfully, off I trooped to the master's study. When I got there, Mr Duff didn't seem to be angry at all. In fact, he appeared to be quite the opposite.

'Ricardo,' he began. 'Worcestershire would like to offer you a summer contract to play for them. This would mean, of course, if you decide to accept it, that your flight home would be cancelled, and you wouldn't be able to return to Barbados until the Christmas holidays.'

This was a lot to take in.

'Yes, I will accept,' I said, surprising myself with how decisive I'd been.

'Good,' said Mr Duff. 'I will make the necessary arrangements and make a phone call to your mother to tell her you won't be coming home for the summer.'

Excitedly, I ran down to the study to tell Gary, and he in turn told the whole house. Soon, I was getting congratulations from the other boys and some of the masters too.

The end of term couldn't come quickly enough; I had come to England to further my education and hopefully get an opportunity to develop my cricketing skills. I'd just passed my 16th birthday, and it was coming together nicely. The contract offer from Worcestershire duly arrived, and I was called into the housemaster's study to read and sign it. Mr Duff explained I would be living in digs in Worcester, adding, 'That's a room in someone else's house,' as he could see I was unfamiliar with the term.

During the last few days of the term, the older boys had all finished their 'O' and 'A' levels, and school was very relaxed as boys began to pack for the summer holidays. However, each morning I was getting increasingly excited as I rushed to get to the newspapers to see how Worcestershire were doing in the County Championship.

Eventually, 12 July arrived, a date that so many at the school had been looking forward to. The place was buzzing with anticipation and excitement as friends said goodbye to each other. Tom was spending the summer at his dad's farm in Worcester, and Gary was getting one of the buses to London to stay with a friend for a few days before catching a flight to Zambia. He had been the first to get up and get dressed before shouting that the buses were outside. They all had signs on them – Paddington, Gerrards Cross, Manchester and Birmingham. Gary was the first to leave. He wished me the best of luck with the cricket as he boarded. I waved and watched him go before returning to the house. A few boys were still there, but Mr Duff asked me to bring my stuff through to the private side and have lunch with him and his family. We then stood by the window and watched the boys leave. Some were picked up in huge cars driven by chauffeurs. I suspected I might be the poorest boy in the school.

Whilst my mind was wandering into all sorts of dark recesses, Mr Duff snapped me out of it with a chirpy, 'Time to go, Ricardo!' I grabbed my bag and walked out to the green Renault in the drive. Sheila and Claire came to the door to say goodbye.

Bags packed and seat belts fastened, off we went, the start of another new adventure.

CHAPTER 7

FROM CLASSROOM TO DRESSING ROOM

The streets and houses became less familiar as we travelled further and further from Malvern. Before long, we turned into Calgary Drive and pulled up outside number 11. The house wasn't as big as School House. Still, it was much bigger than anything in my village. Apprehensively, I got my things out of the boot whilst Mr Duff went and knocked on the door. A dog started barking, and when Mr Duff beckoned me to approach the house, I was reluctant to get any closer. The door opened, and a small dog rushed toward me, causing me to drop my bags and run off down the street. A woman's voice shouted, 'Popsy, Popsy,' as I ran away. Turning, I saw the dog had been picked up, and the lady and Mr Duff were laughing. This was my new landlady, and what I thought was one house was two. Miss Collins gave me a quick tour of the property, taking me upstairs to show me my room whilst pointing out the bathroom and toilet. In the kitchen, she kindly told me it was OK to help myself to everything. However, I wasn't taking much in, as I was still distracted by the dog. Eventually, she put Popsy down, and it immediately started barking. Despite reassurances that the dog had never bitten anyone, I wasn't convinced and stayed clear.

Soon, it was time for Mr Duff to return to Malvern and he told me to behave myself and whispered, 'Keep your room tidy and help with the washing up.' I watched him drive away and then chatted with Miss Collins for a while. Sitting beside me, she told me to call her Ann and use the house as my own. She turned the television on and reached across the table for a pack of cigarettes. Silk Cut. They weren't sold in Barbados. As we watched the news together, the phone rang twice quickly. First, it was Michael Clarke. He said he was pleased my schoolwork had gone well in the first term and congratulated me on my contract with Worcestershire. He said he would try to get over and watch as many matches as possible. Then, I spoke to the coach of Worcestershire, the former England all-rounder Basil D'Oliveira. There was a match the following day, and he wanted me to play in it. It would be 40-overs a side, away against Glamorgan at Cardiff. I would be picked up at 9am. I thanked him for ringing, then told Miss Collins my news before racing upstairs to sort my cricket gear.

The next day couldn't come quickly enough. Awake bright and early, I headed for the shower, dressed and rushed downstairs. Miss Collins was already there and asked what I wanted for breakfast. Unsure, I settled on tea and toast before waiting by the door. Suddenly, a car horn beeped. I grabbed my kit bags and said goodbye to Miss Collins, who wished me luck. Outside, standing beside a white MG sports car, was an extremely tall fellow with a lot of very red hair. He introduced himself as David Banks and took my bags. There was no way it could all fit inside the MG's small boot, but David said it wasn't a problem as he crammed the rest onto the back seat.

Cricket gear was stacked up to the roof, and it was all a little bit cramped as we set off. I stiffened my neck muscles every time David braked, fearing an accident. Soon we were on the motorway and going as fast as the MG could carry us, with George Benson blaring out of the speakers. David explained he would have to stop for petrol and get some breakfast. I wondered if we'd have time to get a meal. It wouldn't be good to be late for my first game! 'Breakfast' for us both turned out to be cans of Coke, bags of crisps and sausage rolls. My new team-mate was clearly an expert at driving and eating at the same time. He put the can of Coke between his legs, had his bag of crisps in one hand and the sausage roll in another, keeping the steering wheel straight with his knees. It was an extraordinary start to the day, and I wondered if all county cricket was as hectic as this. The trip to Cardiff took about one and a half hours, and we were the last to arrive, with the others already dressed and practising as we pulled into the car park.

It was my job to unpack the MG. The dressing room was huge and much warmer than Malvern's. Coach D'Oliveira came over, welcomed me and wished me luck. The game was to begin in the early afternoon, so both sides had lunch together before it started. It allowed David to introduce me to all the other members of the team, including Barbadian Vanburn Holder, a former member of the West Indies Test team and a distant relative of Mum's, who had grown up in the same neighbourhood as the Husbands. Vanburn

63

had just retired from first-class cricket and was now coaching the youngsters at Worcester whilst captaining the second team. He sat with me through lunch, and we chatted about people and places we both knew back home. After we had eaten, Vanburn said I would be opening the bowling. I couldn't believe it or think of anything else as the two captains walked to the middle for the toss. I prayed we would be batting first to give me time to compose myself. We were all watching from the dressing room, with my heart pounding as Vanburn began to walk back towards us.

'We're batting, lads.'

It was the news I'd been hoping for; I could relax as the top-order batters began putting their pads on. Looking around at my new team-mates, I noticed a few were smoking, and a couple were eating chocolate. I'd always wondered what went on in a professional dressing room! When we left, the captain asked if I wanted to have a walk around the boundary edge. I thought it seemed more like an instruction than a question, so I happily went along as he talked about bowling in English conditions. Vanburn explained that because today's game was only 40 overs, getting wickets was less of an issue than stopping runs. He suggested I bowl full and straight because it would be easier for him to set the field. Whilst we completed our walk, the runs flowed freely, and Worcestershire looked on course for a big score. I was told I would bat at number nine, but secretly hoped I wouldn't be needed. Indeed, that's how it turned out, as we made 220 for six.

Tea was taken between innings, giving me plenty of time to put my boots on and think about what was to come. I could feel my nerves building. Then it was time. We all walked down the steps onto the field, and I noticed my hands shaking. Vanburn gave me the ball, 'Just give it your best shot.' I was determined not to let myself or my team down and began to mark out my full run, only to be told there were limited run-ups in these matches. Annoyed that I hadn't spotted it earlier or that nobody had mentioned it, I just hoped I could do what I wanted to do from a shorter run. The first two balls were wides, hardly the best start to my Worcestershire career. Vanburn came over from mid-off and said to take my time and concentrate on bowling straight. Those few words helped, and my confidence began to grow. I was able to increase my pace, and by the end of my eight-over spell, I had taken 2-24. It wasn't the six or seven wickets I'd hoped for, but I was pleased nonetheless, and everyone seemed happy for me. Worcestershire won the game easily enough, so I felt it had gone OK.

After the game, everyone moved to the bar for a drink before it was time to load up the MG. Somehow, it seemed we had even more stuff for the return journey. The trip back to Worcester was quite jovial, and David even had time for a race up the motorway with one of the other players. Once we were back in Worcester, David decided to stop at a pub. He said he would show me round the town and perhaps we'd go on to a nightclub later. I wasn't so sure. I was not too fond of the taste of beer, but David insisted I try one. We were in the Angel Place part of town at a pub called The Shakespeare, and we stayed there until almost 11pm when David said it was time to go. We drove the short distance to a nightclub called Tramps, tucked away down a back street. Inside, the music was deafening, and I couldn't help but notice how many women were there; most seemed to know David. It was quite a night, and I enjoyed it the longer it went on... which was until 2am, as it turns out. David took me back to Miss Collins' house and announced he would pick me up at 9am tomorrow. It was a good job it was only for net practice! I laid in bed and thought about the day's events; I hadn't felt out of my depth at any stage and enjoyed being around county cricketers. If this was to be a substantial part of my life, then I was very much looking forward to it.

In what seemed like a matter of moments, I was up but felt full of energy and eager to see what the new day would bring. Miss Collins had a cautionary word for me as she made breakfast, telling me if I were to make it as a professional sportsman, then I would need all the sleep I could get. She had remained awake, listening for my return and, in her words, 'praying that nothing bad had happened.' I apologised and assured her it had been a one-off.

Then, the white MG arrived. It was only a matter of ten minutes or so before we were at the County Ground and unloading our kit. Some of the senior players had sponsored cars, and I noticed a BMW with the name BASIL D'OLIVEIRA written on the door. I stood for a moment, trying to envisage the day I had my name on a sponsored car, and everyone would know who I was and wave at me as I went past. David led me up the stairs to the dressing room and introduced me to a grey-haired gentleman, 'Jack, the Old Bastard.' He was the dressing room attendant and was clearly used to getting a ribbing from some of the players. He just said, 'Hiya duck,' to me as I shook his hand. I looked around and noticed a door marked PHYSIO, through which emerged a man who David introduced as 'Pinkie the Physio.' The dressing room appeared so large, with plenty of lockers with players' names on them and a huge table in the centre that had three or four bats on it. There was a television, a fridge and a huge bottle of orange juice in the room. I was wondering where to put my stuff, and David said, 'Not here, we're upstairs. This is for the first team; they're all away playing in Yorkshire.' So, I followed him up the narrow wooden staircase and began to hear voices, some of which I recognised from the previous day. The players welcomed me into the room, and pretty soon we were all playing a mini-game of cricket with a stump and a tennis ball. There was lots of laughter, but suddenly someone yelled for us to stop. Footsteps could be heard climbing the steps, and then a slightly balding head appeared over the banister. It was the coach, Basil D'Oliveira. Immediately, it was down to business. 'I want the opening batsmen padded up and ready in the nets at 10am,' he boomed.

On the outfield, for the first time, I took in what a beautiful ground it was. I'd often seen pictures of New Road when reading about county cricket. Ahead of me, the other players were wandering across the ground towards the far corner, where the nets were situated. As I walked, I glanced around and spotted all of the advertising boards surrounding the boundary. To the right of the pavilion was a sign: 'Ladies Pavilion.' I wondered if ladies' cricket was also played on the ground, and I then noticed the beautiful old scoreboard with the cathedral in the background.

Reaching the practice area, I deposited my kit at the back of the nets and heard the coach asking us all to warm up. I followed some of the others on a gentle run towards the edge of the river and observed a small boat go by before we stopped and did some stretching. There was an artificial surface, but the coach wanted me to bowl with a new ball in one of the grass nets. It lasted about two hours, and I felt in good rhythm, although no one said too much. I wondered what would happen next, but everyone collected their kit and returned to the pavilion. Inside, David told me we would now be going to 'The Shakespeare' for lunch. It seemed like a race as he told me to get into the car quickly. So away we went; once or twice he even mounted the footpath, and on one occasion, I'm sure he went the wrong way down a one-way street; but his shortcut meant we arrived first.

The landlord and landlady of the pub, Graham and Sheila, had already laid out a few tables, and it was clear this was a regular arrangement. A few players went to the gambling machines while shouting their food orders across the bar. Photographs of teams and players adorned the pub's walls, with other bits of cricket memorabilia strategically placed. Whilst we ate, there was lots of chat about the morning's practice, and then suddenly, everyone was rushing again to the afternoon session. I ran in and bowled for two more hours, although things eased down and were gentler in the final hour. I was shattered and wondered if every day would be like this. All I wanted to do was have a shower and get some sleep. Thinking we were done, I laid on the grass, but almost immediately, the coach asked us onto the main ground for fielding drills. By now, I was completely cooked and very much regretting the excesses of the previous evening. Every muscle in my body ached, and even walking was an effort. Jack came up the stairs and could immediately see how stiff I was. He said, if you come down in 15 minutes, I will have a nice Radox bath ready for you. It was exactly what I needed, and I laid there for a long time feeling totally relaxed. Back upstairs in the dressing room, David said all the boys would be hitting the town. I couldn't believe anyone would want to go out after a session like that and said I'd prefer to go home. David obviously had plans. We couldn't leave until he'd brushed his teeth for about 15 minutes, combed and re-combed his hair several times and then splashed on an extraordinary amount of Paco Rabanne aftershave. I was so glad to be dropped off and didn't even mind Popsy jumping up and barking as I walked in. Miss Collins was sunbathing in the garden, so I put my kit away and went straight up to bed.

Pulling the blanket back, I kicked off my shoes and dropped into bed, fully clothed or, as my dad would say, 'I went to bed formal'. I must have slept soundly because the next thing I was aware of was Popsy barking at 8.30am. I was still fully clothed from the previous day at breakfast, and I could tell Miss Collins was suspicious. 'Did you stay out all night?' she asked. I explained I'd seen her sunbathing and hadn't wanted to disturb her but was so tired after practice I'd gone straight to bed. She just smiled. The previous day's routine had already begun by the time we arrived at the ground. Breakfast snacks were scattered around the dressing room, and the coach's arrival again interrupted the stump and tennis ball game. Mr Duff had arranged for me to play for Colwall Cricket Club in the Three Counties League. It seemed all of the second team played for amateur sides at weekends. Whilst I was keen to play matches, I couldn't believe the intensity of it all. I was either playing, practising or travelling. I'd never played so much cricket! Surely, I was bowling myself into the ground? Again, I opted to go home early after the session and shun the town's attractions. Miss Collins had taken a call from Andy Murtagh whilst I'd been out, saying he would pick me up the following day at midday.

CHAPTER 8

LATE NIGHTS AND EARLY MORNINGS

After catching up with some much-needed sleep, I was up and waiting for Andy for our journey to Colwall. The drive took us through Malvern, and it was nice to see how peaceful it appeared without the bustle of hundreds of schoolchildren. Climbing up through the Malvern hills, Andy pulled into a lay-by and pointed out some landmarks. There was the Three Counties Showground, which still had some of the marquees erected, the main college building, and in the distance, we could make out Worcester to the left and Gloucester to the right. Just then, a jet flew past, very close to the ground and disappeared around the other side of the hill. As we drove further up the hill, Andy nodded towards a pub called The Wyche Inne. We eventually reached the top of the hill and began our descent, past the Colwall Hotel and the Horse & Jockey pub. A dirt track took us past the railway line and into a cricket ground, where a small boy came running over and introduced himself as Paul, the scorer. He asked if he could help with my cricket gear, promptly took my bat, and ran towards a small shed in the corner of the field. As I walked across, I could see some horses galloping in the field next door and noticed a handful of people starting to spread their picnics on the boundary edge. The shed was the dressing room, and everyone moved up to make room as it was pretty tight inside. Andy introduced me to the captain, Adrian Berry, who was tall and had a shock of red hair. Next to him was another redhead, Nick Berry and outside the window was Richard Berry, who also had red hair. I wondered if the whole team was made up of Berrys with red hair!

Colwall, I was told, were lying mid-table in the Three Counties League, and I sensed everyone was hoping I might be able to make a difference. The opponents were Ross-on-Wye, who were placed just above Colwall. Our captain won the toss and inserted the opposition; it proved a good decision. I picked up five wickets as we bowled them out for 114 and then watched Andy Murtagh score a few runs before I managed a quick 20 to win the match. The mood was very jovial in the bar afterwards as players and supporters revelled in the victory. It was very noisy, with lots of laughter, people talking loudly, babies crying, and dogs barking. A victory can make such a difference in a team sports environment, with even one or two suggesting this might be the year Colwall could win the Three Counties League for the first time.

There was another match the following day, against Hereford, the reigning champions and current league leaders. Andy explained there had been a change of plan and instead of returning to Miss Collins, I would be staying with the captain. We had a few more drinks at the club before the whole party moved to the Horse & Jockey, a very old pub full of pictures of past Derby and Grand National winners. We talked late into the evening before returning to Adrian's house, five minutes away. His wife, Kath, was still awake.

Early the following day, I was awoken by a rumble of thunder. Looking out of the window, I was slightly puzzled because the sun was shining brightly. Then it happened again...

It wasn't thunder; it was a high-speed jet passing by!

Kath made me a delicious breakfast, which I devoured, and we set off for the ground. The opposing team were already practising. Andy arrived with his wife and mentioned Mr Duff would be up later to watch the game. Adrian pointed out the opening batter he most wanted to get out. It was one of my Worcestershire team-mates.

Hereford got off to a good start, but I eventually made the breakthrough, and once the opening bat had gone, the rest folded quickly and I'd taken another five wickets. Once the runs had been knocked off, the bar was again buzzing. Everyone was sure this was going to be Colwall's year. Andy drove me back to Miss Collins. I re-lived each of the ten wickets I'd taken over the weekend and prayed I'd continue to enjoy similar successes for Worcestershire.

A beeping car horn woke me the following morning. I took a second to gather my senses. It was 9.30am. Through the blinds, I could see the MG and David waving up at me. I yelled I was on my way and got ready in a mad rush, running out of the door with kit in one hand and shoes in another. David ensured we arrived at the ground on time; the dressing room game with the stump was already underway. The coach appeared as usual and asked everyone how they had got on over the weekend.

One by one, they answered until it was my turn. 'Five wickets both days, coach,' I proudly announced. We learned the net session would be relatively short because we would be playing a match at the Royal Grammar School the following day while Worcestershire's first team would be playing Warwickshire at New Road in the second round of the NatWest Trophy. After practice, David explained we could go out for a drink, as the following day's match wasn't that important for us. He took ages getting ready before saying you should, 'sharpen up because you'll never pull in those.' I didn't know what he meant as I was already wearing my smartest clothes. I couldn't imagine what I could wear that would be smarter. David was always exceptionally well turned out and didn't smell too bad either. Searching my belongings, I came across a bell-bottom pair of trousers I hadn't worn for a long time. I sprayed myself with some of Miss Collins' perfume and scampered down the stairs for David's approval. He was sitting reading the *Worcester Evening News* but looked up at me, standing in my cream-coloured bell-bottoms and grandad shirt. He burst into laughter. 'I suggest you save some of your meal allowances and get yourself some new threads!'

Our first stopping point was the Horn & Trumpet, better known as the Horn and Crumpet, where David introduced me to a few girls. Before long, we were joined by several team-mates, and at closing time, the whole party moved on to La Trek nightclub. It was very lively, and I enjoyed a couple of lagers. I was looking forward to heading back to my bed when I noticed a very attractive blonde girl sitting at the bar. I asked David if he knew her, and he asked if I wanted an introduction. Armed with some Dutch courage, I replied I was perfectly capable of introducing myself and started to walk over. However, I quickly changed my mind and asked David to do the honours. Her name was Julie. David told her I would be the new cricket superstar. I bought her a drink, and then the slow music started; she took my hand and led me to the dance floor. This was a whole new experience, but I tried to copy what others were doing and pretended I'd done it all my life. Julie noticed me looking towards David, who was dancing with a girl I'd not seen before. 'That's my sister, Debbie,' she said. The two girls looked at each other and smiled.

When the music stopped playing at 2am, David offered both girls a lift home. Julie and I were cramped together in the back of the MG while Debbie sat in the front, with the seat as far forward as possible. It wasn't far to the girls' house, but I was in agony with cramps, and we had to stop for a stretch to get rid of it. It was apparent that David had been to the house before, a semi-detached south of the city. Debbie asked if anyone would like coffee, and David accepted. The girls' tones had become very hushed, and when they were both in the kitchen, David explained that their mother was upstairs. The two girls eventually returned, and Debbie sat beside David on the sofa. Julie returned to the kitchen to fetch the biscuits. As soon as Julie was gone, David and Debbie started kissing passionately. I felt very uncomfortable sitting there, so I decided to help Julie with the biscuits. We sat in the kitchen and chatted until there was a knock on the door. It was David, wanting to know if I was ready to leave. He gave Debbie another kiss, and as I said good night to Julie, I leaned forward, and we kissed. The streets were quiet, and soon we were outside Miss Collins' house. By now, it was 4am, and David asked if he could sleep on the sofa instead of going home. I climbed the stairs and was asleep within minutes.

The next day when I came down, David was playing with Popsy and Miss Collins was setting up the video machine, explaining she was going to be out all day. David and I stopped at the garage for breakfast and watched everyone walking with their picnics and umbrellas towards New Road. Worcestershire versus Warwickshire is a local derby, and the ground would be full. Traffic was at a standstill, and I wished I could be playing in such an important match. Instead, our destination was the nearby Royal Grammar School. There were pictures of famous players on the wall; one looked familiar. David confirmed it was Imran Khan, the Pakistan Test captain, who had been a pupil there and played for Worcestershire before joining Sussex.

The match was light-hearted; players even drew straws to determine their batting positions. Worcester batted first and everyone was expected to either retire or get out as soon as they had scored 50, but David carried on and scored a hundred, to jeers from the other players. I bowled five overs and picked up a wicket, but it was one of those occasions when everyone was given a chance to bowl. The match finished fairly early, but the night before was catching up with me, so I decided to go straight home.

The following day we were playing Somerset at New Road. David phoned early in the morning to say the MG had broken down and he couldn't pick me up. Miss Collins explained a bus from Malvern passed through every hour and would drop me near the ground. Despite my best efforts, I missed it. With the next bus an hour away, I decided to walk. I hoped someone would stop and give me a lift. Where was the Prime Minister when I needed him? Car after car went by without stopping, and I walked all the way to the ground. The other players were already in the nets, so I changed quickly. Several of the first team were in the main dressing room as I walked through, and I recognised a few, having read about them or seen them on television. I couldn't believe I was in the same dressing room as Alan Ormrod, Dipak Patel and Norman Gifford. They were chatting and seemed oblivious as I passed. When I reached the practice area, I was confronted by the coach, asking where I'd been. My explanation didn't cut any ice, and I was told to allow myself more time in future as there was no excuse for being late. Just then, David arrived and was given the same ticking off. We were in the field first, and I wondered if some of those first-team players might be watching. Perhaps I let my concentration slide as a result, and I had a poor session, but everyone was very supportive at lunch, and my performance improved afterwards.

Drained, I went straight home at the end of the day and had another early night. I'd been disappointed with how it had gone but knew we'd been up against a strong Somerset side. The remaining two days of the match went a lot better, and I even managed a couple of good wickets, boosting my confidence for my next game with Colwall the following day. For a small village club, Colwall always managed to attract a good crowd. So now, with a chance of challenging for the title, the place was packed for the two weekend games. Both were convincingly won, but the news came through Hereford had also won and remained top of the table, with Colwall in second so the return fixture between the top two would be a crunch match.

The following week, I received my first pay packet from Worcestershire for £50. I thought this was more money than I could ever possibly spend. David was immediately on at me to buy some new clothes so we went into the shopping centre, and I chose a new outfit. I felt I was going to be irresistible in my new threads.

The weekend brought more success for Colwall, and we moved to the top of the table for the first time. However, my weekly successes with them brought issues. Worcestershire's committee had been watching my progress and felt the gap between the Three Counties League and second XI county cricket was too large. They felt I was perhaps finding my weekend cricket a little too easy and thought I should challenge myself more. So, the decision was made for me to transfer to Worcester City Cricket Club in the Birmingham League. Whilst I enjoyed the new challenge and made some new friends, I was disappointed for Colwall. They lost a few games after I left and finished third. It was higher than they'd ever managed previously, but who knows if I'd been allowed to stay with them until the end? Maybe we'd have won the league.

All too soon, it was time to say goodbye to my Worcestershire team-mates and head back to Malvern for the autumn term. It was a sad time, especially knowing some players were going off around the world to continue playing. David was heading to Perth for the winter and promised to write. Back at the house, I thanked Miss Collins for looking after me before Mr Duff arrived for my return to college. All I could think about was whether I'd done enough to impress and be invited back the following summer. What a summer it had been, from cans of Coke, crisps and sausage rolls for breakfast on the way to games to the odd weekend spent with the mother of my guardian, Michael Clarke, in posh surroundings, where jacket and tie were worn for dinner. The college was very quiet as the other boys wouldn't be back until Sunday evening, so I had two days on my own to reflect.

Over the rest of the weekend, more and more boys were dropped off, and excited chatter began to fill the air, with everyone keen to know what their friends had been up to. I made the most of the relaxed rules and watched as much television as possible. By supper time on Sunday, everyone was back. Mr Duff welcomed everyone and congratulated several people on their 'O' and 'A' level results, with a kind word for those who had failed. Duff then explained what he expected of the boys during the coming term. As I approached our study, I could hear the unmistakable sound of The Jam blaring out. In a way, I'd missed this, an almost endless loop of 'Going Underground', 'Eton Rifles', 'Town called Malice', 'Down at the Tube

Station at Midnight', and so on. The boys packed their things away, shouting loudly over the music. Then suddenly, we became aware of a presence. The door opened slowly, and there was the chuckle. I'd not heard it for weeks but instantly knew it was Mr Duff. Andrew reached quickly for the volume control, but it was too late. Mr Duff had given enough warnings in the past about the loud music, and now it was going to be confiscated for two weeks. Duff calmly unplugged the system while discussing the summer holidays and then asked Andrew for help taking it to his study. Andrew couldn't believe he had to help to take his own stereo away. Returning to the study, he sat doing funny impersonations of Mr Duff puffing on his pipe and chuckling.

Lights went out at ten, and whilst the others chatted away, I thought about Mum and how much I missed her. I must have fallen asleep and was dreaming about her in church, with the bells ringing. Suddenly I realised it wasn't a dream or a church bell – it was the alarm. Time to get up.

The routine had begun once again. A routine that started with me putting on trousers and a blazer. It had been so long since I had worn them that I'd almost forgotten the feeling. A Coke and sausage roll breakfast with David was replaced by scrambled eggs on toast, followed by plenty of toast and marmalade. Then it was assembly. I'd often considered dodging it but knew I'd be missed immediately. It's easy to notice when the only black boy in school isn't there.

The familiar rhythm of the school day returned, and I only had the occasional cricket net to look forward to. Football was the primary sport at this time of year, and I played in a few of the house matches, did a bit of basketball, swam when I could, and did some weightlifting. The weather worsened as the term went on, so I thought I'd try some indoor sports too. Academically, Mr Duff helped me catch up with the others in mathematics and physics, but I still needed extra tutoring for subjects such as history and English literature. The days became shorter, and I couldn't believe I was living in a country where it was getting dark by 3pm in winter. My thoughts drifted increasingly towards Barbados, and I wrote many letters to my family and Joyce. The closer it got to Christmas, the more I thought about going home, and finally, I plucked up the courage to approach Mr Duff about it. Fortunately, he felt it was the right decision to go home, realising how much I was missing it. Plans were put in place, and a few days later, Mr Duff showed me a plane ticket for 13 December. It was still about a month away, but I could think of nothing else for the remainder of the day. That night I wrote a long letter to Mum and Joyce, giving them the good news. I fell asleep thinking of whether Barbados had changed. Who would collect me from the airport? Would Joyce still be happy to see me?

I awoke to find it had snowed heavily overnight. It was about 7am, but it looked like early evening, it was so dark. After breakfast, I looked outside at some of the boys having snowball fights. I decided to give that a miss, grabbed my books, and ran towards the main college. Approaching the back door, I stopped suddenly and lost my footing, falling heavily. Picking myself slowly up, I was aware I was covered in snow, and people were laughing at me. My books, pens, and ink fillers were everywhere.

I felt so embarrassed and was grateful to Gary, who helped gather my stuff before leading me to the toilets, where I could clean myself. When I finally made it into class, everyone had already heard and there was more laughter. That incident marred the whole day, and when I finally got to bed, I was keener than ever to get back to Barbados to be with my family.

The following morning Mr Duff came into breakfast and asked to see me in his study. I wondered what I'd done; could it be about my fall the previous day?

He told me Laker Airways had gone into receivership. I didn't understand so he explained it had run into financial difficulties. So basically, all their flights had been cancelled. I couldn't believe it. Yesterday, I had fallen over, and today my flight home had been cancelled.

CHAPTER 9

GONE A BOY, BACK A MAN

Near to tears, I walked back to our study, hoping I'd still be able to get home, hopefully before 13 December. The next couple of days dragged, and every time I saw Mr Duff, I expected him to give me news, but he seemed to ignore me. Growing increasingly anxious, I began scouring the newspapers and saw a report in *The Times* saying other airlines were helping Laker's customers get to their destinations. I took this as a positive and began packing my things in expectation. I was sitting in the study when the door slowly opened, and in walked Mr Duff.

'Your flight has been confirmed for 13 December. It leaves from Gatwick but has a stop in Amsterdam.'

I wrote to Mum and Joyce, telling them the good news, even though I knew I might get there before the letters. Arrangements were made for me to stay with Tony Richardson, a boy from the year below, for the night before my flight. He lived in Redhill, ten minutes from Gatwick.

It was an excited bunch of schoolchildren who were outside awaiting the coaches on the morning of our departure. They hadn't arrived when I took my bags down, but Tony was there, and I promised to join him shortly. First, I went to the private side to see Mr Duff, who had my plane ticket and a letter for Mum. I said goodbye to him and his wife and returned to join the others. In 24 hours, I would be airborne, returning to Barbados. Would Mum see a difference in me? Would she think I'd changed? I couldn't wait to see her.

We were heading to a drop-off point at Gerrard's Cross, where Tony's dad would meet us. As we joined the M5, I couldn't help but think about my experiences with Worcestershire's second XI; it seemed to revolve around the M5. Eventually, we turned off and headed towards Oxford. I joined some of the others in a game of cards but was distracted by the roar of a couple of fighter jets. They disappeared over the trees towards the RAF Brize Norton airbase, Gary said. We eventually reached our destination, and I gasped at the line of cars waiting. Aston Martins, BMWs, Jaguars, Mercedes, and a Rolls-Royce. The coach emptied as the boys ran to their loved ones, and I proceeded to get my cases and wait for Tony. Gary came over and we said our goodbyes and wished each other Happy Christmas. Tony then led me to a red BMW 635 and introduced me to his dad, Brian. I got into the car and was immediately taken by the strong smell of leather. Looking out the window, I spotted Neil, a boy from my year, putting his bags into the boot of the Rolls Royce. We set off, but Brian drove a short distance and pulled up alongside the Rolls Royce to speak to Neil's dad.

'How's business?' he asked.

'A little slow, but we expect things to pick up,' came the reply.

They chatted for a few moments about golf before we headed off. Brian asked if I knew who that man was. He explained he was Ian MacLaurin , chairman of Tesco, one of the biggest supermarket chains in Great Britain. They had been pupils at Malvern, along with my sponsor, Mr Clarke.

Tony's mum, Elaine, and his two sisters, Sarah and Zoe, were waiting for us. It was warm, spacious, and a big log fire was burning, just as I'd imagined all English houses to be. Elaine showed me to my room, and after dinner I was shown around, firstly to the indoor swimming pool and then to the stables to see the ponies. Brian chatted to me about cricket and mentioned he'd played briefly for Warwickshire after school but now turned out for Wimbledon on Saturdays and the Old Malvernians on Sundays.

I grew increasingly excited about my journey home, so it was with some relief that I got to bed. They'd allocated me a spare room, which also had a television, so I flicked through the stations looking for something to watch. On one of the channels I came across Jimmy Tarbuck. I thought his jokes were hilarious and hoped I'd remember some of them to tell everyone at home.

Up bright and early, I washed myself in the pink bath; I didn't know they made other colours apart from white. I was dressed by the time Brian knocked to say breakfast was ready. Tony, his sisters, and their mum were off to London for Christmas shopping, so it would be Brian driving me to the airport. I was flying with the Dutch airline Martinair. After passing through passport control, I still had an hour before my flight so I looked around the duty-free shops, intending to buy a box of chocolates for Mum and perhaps a Walkman for myself. I was so engrossed I lost track of time and was startled to hear over the tannoy, 'This is the final call for Martinair Flight 130 to Amsterdam and Bridgetown, Barbados. Boarding at Gate 51.' The airport was large and I had no idea where Gate 51 was and ran around frantically. Finally, a lady pointed me to an escalator and said I should look for the number at the top. It seemed to take forever, but I got there in the nick of time. Finally, I was on my way home! The engines became noisier and noisier, and I was pushed back into my seat as it gathered speed. Suddenly, the aircraft braked sharply, and everyone was left straining forward, held in place by their seat belts. One or two people began screaming. We taxied gently back to the terminal building, and I felt sure I wasn't going home after all.

Then, a voice came over the intercom, 'Good morning, ladies and gentlemen; this is the captain speaking. Sorry for the false start, but during the take-off run, we noticed a problem with the navigational system, so we aborted to sort it out but we do expect to be lining up again very soon.'

Soon enough, we were airborne, first to Amsterdam and then to Barbados. Alongside me were a couple from Manchester, who said it was their first time abroad. They hadn't been on holiday for two years and usually went to Devon, but they were venturing further now that their children had grown up and left home. I told them about Barbados, where to go for the best beaches, what to eat, and where to shop. Time dragged but eventually the captain announced we were descending into Bridgetown, where the local time was 5pm and the temperature 84 degrees. There was a cheer from some of the passengers, and I wondered who would be there to greet me.

We landed, and getting off the plane, I could make out my dad straightaway, standing at the bottom of the ramp. Ovey was there too, but that was to be expected as he was a customs officer. I was first off the plane, and there were lots of people shouting and waving. Dad seemed so pleased to see me. 'That's my son,' he beamed. 'He's come from England, and the drinks are on me tonight.' He told me Mum was there too but waiting on the other side of customs. So, through a sliding door we went and there on the other side was my mum. Alongside her were Dale, Alison, and cousin Christine, who was now living with the family. Before I could speak, Mum hugged and kissed me, and she wouldn't let go of me, exclaiming I looked a little paler. She was wearing a woollen jumper because she felt cold. I said she should try England, where it was -10 degrees.

Like our journey out some nine months before, everyone had come to the airport in a minibus, and the music was blaring. My mum appeared in shock, almost as if she couldn't accept that I was back beside her. She said I'd grown a few inches and had filled out a little. As we set off, I had to readjust, as the roads seemed narrower now compared to those I'd gotten used to in the UK. The one thing I enjoyed was the lovely warm air. The moon reflected off the ocean, and there were plenty of tourists about; the island was in full party mode. Moving inland, there were no streetlights, and the roads were pitted with bumps and potholes, but the driver did his best to dodge them. Before long, I could see the outskirts of Redman's Village, and a few friends I recognised sat chatting outside the mini-market. The houses seemed much smaller than before I'd left, but Pearl's shop was still there. We pulled up outside, and Dad shouted that everyone was welcome to come over to the house.

'Ricky's back!'

Someone had given the house a lick of paint since I'd last seen it, and the surrounds had been weeded. That was a job I had always hated doing, and I was thankful I wouldn't be doing it again any time soon.

Dad was throwing the doors open to host a 'Welcome Home party' and as I got out of the minibus, more and more people came over to say hello. Eunice and Ossie were looking through their window, so I went to see them. Eunice hugged me and said, 'I prayed to the Lord to bring you home safely.' We chatted briefly, and then I returned to the chatter and the booming music from our house. The first tangible sign I'd grown was when I had to stoop to enter the doorway. Family and friends were laughing and having a good time; food and drink were plentiful. 'I'm going to party until New Year's Day and drink from wine to iodine,' Dad said. Everyone came and wanted to know about England, and the party went on through the early hours of the morning, with the last guest leaving at around 5am. Dale, Alison, and Christine had gone to bed, and Dad was fast asleep on the sofa. That left just Mum and me; she came, sat on my bed and asked what it was like at Malvern.

'What were the other boys like?'

'How did the masters treat you?'

'How big was the school?'

'What was the lady you spent the summer with like?'

I answered as much as I could, but it had been a long day, and I was tired and soon fell asleep. The bright early sun woke me, and whilst I would have liked a little more sleep, I heard the others up and about. I was looking forward to some proper Barbadian home cooking. Breakfast was fried plantain and fish cakes, and as it was Sunday, Mum had already started to prepare lunch. Smells wafted around the house; I'd dreamt of rice and peas with beef stew several times while I'd been away, and now, first day back, that's what we were having. My plans for the day involved getting in touch with Joyce and letting her know I was back. Perhaps she had found someone else in my absence. Twice I dialled her number before putting the phone down. I wasn't sure what I wanted to say and was concerned she wouldn't want to talk to me. Plucking up the courage, I dialled again; it rang two or three times, and someone answered before slamming down the receiver. Irrational thoughts ran through my mind. Did she know it was me? How could she? I tried the number again, and this time she answered. Gently, I asked if she knew who was calling.

'Sure, I do,' she laughed. 'It's Ricky. I have a friend in Redman's Village who told me you got back last night.' I asked her why she'd put the phone down on me, and she said her daughter had been playing with the phone and got to it first. Aware that Mum was making a special effort with the dinner and was expecting me to be there, I told Joyce I'd come and see her a little later, maybe in the evening.

Dad spent the morning at Pearl's and came home just in time for lunch, prompting Mum to call him a great pot-timer. He'd had a few drinks and wasn't too interested in the food, but when he asked about my schoolwork, it reminded me of something. I dashed off and returned with the letter Mr Duff had given for my parents. Mum read it aloud, and it told them everything I'd been doing and was very complimentary about my schoolwork. They both said they were very happy for me, so I took the opportunity to tell them I would be seeing Joyce later. The news didn't go down well with

81

Mum, but Dad was fine and even gave me the bus fare. When it was time to get ready, I went for a shower in the outside bathroom and prayed that one day I would have enough money to buy my parents a bathroom as big and as beautiful as Brian and Elaine's, but maybe not quite as pink!

The bus ride brought back memories of all those trips down to Combermere on school mornings. I began getting anxious as I approached Joyce's house, wondering whether she'd still fancy me. Knocking on the door, I heard a small child crying, and then the door opened. Joyce invited me in and said my skin had got paler since she'd last seen me. We chatted and got on well again; it was easy to remember why I'd fallen in love with her in the first place. We played with Duana, her daughter until it was bedtime. Joyce came back and sat beside me, holding my hand. She kissed my cheek, then my lips. I wasn't sure what I wanted to happen next but told her I ought to be getting back. She told me there was no need; I could stay the night. Confusion reigned; I knew mum would be so angry if I stayed out the night.

I was also wary; all my previous attempts to have sex had been disasters. Sandra had been the same age as me when we sneaked through the sugar cane and away from the sports day at the National Stadium to try to have sex, but we were then so scared that we might get caught. Then there was Ann-Marie, a classmate. That was a failure. And it was the same with Kathy, who lived next door. Joyce was more experienced than any of them but said she hadn't been with anyone since Duana's father had left her. What would I tell Mum tomorrow, or should I turn up and say nothing? Joyce led me into the bedroom and… well, what should I say? This beautiful woman, sensing my nerves, reassured me she couldn't get pregnant. We removed our clothes, and then she helped me through the process and then helped me through it a couple more times before we both drifted off into a deep, blissful sleep.

Duana's crying woke us up, and I immediately panicked about what I would tell Mum. I stayed and had breakfast with Joyce and hoped my parents had gone to work by the time I returned. Promising to call her later, I jumped on the No.2 bus back to the village. All the people walking around seemed to be looking at me, and I thought they must know I'd stayed out and made love for the first time. No one was home, but it wasn't long before I spied Mum walking up the street. She looked particularly angry, but she walked into the room and didn't say a word. When Dad came home, he asked me outright what had happened, so I explained I'd missed the last bus and had to stay with a friend. He wasn't fooled and had a little chuckle to himself.

Over the next few days, I returned to my old routine, playing plenty of tennis ball cricket in the road and taking a few sea baths. As the weekend approached, I realised I would have to tell more lies to get away and spend time with Joyce. So, I decided to say I was going to spend some time with a friend on the north coast of the island. Seizing my moment between chats about Malvern and Worcestershire, I mentioned I was going to St Lucy with Hendy, something I'd done many times before. 'I hope you're not sleeping with a woman, Ricky,' said Mum. The subject was quickly changed because Dad arrived with his Sony radio, listening to the cricket. West Indies were playing Australia in Brisbane, and as they were doing pretty well. We sat up together and listened until late into the night.

Rising early, I packed a few things into a bag and waited a discreet amount of time after breakfast before heading off, barely hearing a final warning of 'I hope you are being smart, Ricky.' The rest of that weekend will live with me forever. By day we played with Duana and watched television together, and at night Joyce and I spent hours getting to know each other better. Whereas she had all the experience, I was a fast learner! It felt right when I told her, 'I loved you'. She replied, 'I love you too, Ricky.'

All too soon, it was time to say goodbye, and I hoped there would be no explaining to do. That seemed unlikely because as soon as I walked through the door, Mum asked how Hendy was. I said he was OK and made a mental note to warn Hendy about my lie in case Mum should bump into him. But she was preoccupied with something... and that something turned out to be Dad's drinking. He'd promised, in his usual forthright manner, he would 'drink from wine to iodine' whilst I was home, and he seemed to be trying to do just that. Every night he was out until late, drinking with his mates, and now it was becoming an issue between my parents. Earlier in the year, doctors had warned Dad about his rising blood pressure and advised him to reduce his alcohol intake. He had laughed, saying, 'It's because the doctor wants to drink it all for himself.' He had a theory that boiling breadfruit leaves and sipping the watery residue would lower his blood pressure, so this was becoming a normal thing to do before going on drinking sessions. Whenever Mum confronted him, the reply had always been about me. 'Ricky's back for Christmas, so I will enjoy it to the fullest.'

It went on like this until a couple of days before Christmas. The house was starting to smell of seasonal treats. All the windows were washed, dried, and then shined with newspaper, and I helped spread crushed grit around the house as pretend snow. On Christmas Eve, a large ham was taken from the roof, where it had been hanging for the past month and put in a tub to soak in readiness for cooking. A fruit mixture was removed from the cupboard, where it had been fermenting since the previous Christmas. New curtains were fitted, a Christmas tree and lights were put up, and an array of cakes and sponges were baked alongside the main Christmas cake that was pungent enough to make you drunk with just one sniff. I loved everything about Christmas and couldn't wait for the big day.

Everyone was up early on Christmas morning to discover presents had magically appeared under the tree. I remember a mad scramble to see which presents belonged to whom and the sheer delight when we opened new matching tracksuits. I'd managed to hide the big box of assorted chocolates I'd bought at Gatwick and brought them out for everyone to try. No one wanted a typical breakfast, and although Mum wasn't happy, we each ate one of her sponges. Dad began preparing the ham. For as long as I could remember, that had been his job, to cook the Christmas ham, and he took great pride in it, although it also meant he could stay behind while the rest of us went off to church. Dale and I were always restless through the service and pleased when it was over, so we could return to enjoy our presents. Back at the house, Dad was dealing with the ham and Mum began preparing the rest of the meal. Sporting our new tracksuits, Dale and I decided to go out and have a game of cricket, but we had no fielders. We begged Alison and Christine, but they refused until we offered money. No sooner had we started than boys began arriving from all over the village. The girls seemed upset when we told them they weren't needed and more so when they were told they wouldn't be paid! The game continued until we were called in for our Christmas lunch. Other family members had arrived by now to join the feast. Apart from the ham, there was rice, green peas, macaroni pie, potato pie, chicken, pork, beef stew and jug-jug, a little bit of everything ground together as a stuffing. Everyone drank sorrel, a very red drink made from a native Barbadian plant which is boiled, drained and sweetened.

Eating went way into the night, and then the drinking and the music started. Other villagers came round to chat and share a drink. Tomorrow it would be someone else's house, and someone else's the following day. These parties would go on until New Year's Day. With Christmas falling as it had, Saturday and Sunday were two extra days off work. Dad had made plans to spend Saturday with Denny Luke and Sunday with Shepherd, another of his friends. Whilst Mum was at church on the Sunday morning, I caught the bus into town and went to see Joyce. She packed up a picnic, and we took Duana down to the beach, a walk of around 20 minutes. We sat not too far from the Barbados Hilton and talked about the future. I suggested that when I'd finished college, perhaps, I could get a job in England, and she could join me. She seemed reluctant, having spent her entire life in Barbados. Perhaps if I did make it as a county cricketer, we could become used to spending six months together and six months apart each year. We both promised to think about it. Soon enough, I would have other things to occupy my thoughts, however. My life was about to take its darkest turn yet.

CHAPTER 10

STRUCK DOWN BY GRIEF

Everyone had gone out by the time I returned from Joyce's. Mum had gone to Cousin Norma's for a party, and Alison and Christine had stayed with Haa. Dale had gone over to Shepherd's house with Dad. When I arrived, the party was in full swing, and it was apparent that Dad had been drinking and enjoying himself. Seeing me there, he told everyone a future West Indian player had just arrived. He announced he would be there when I played my first Test match, and all his friends agreed they'd be there too. Everyone sang and danced late into the evening before Dad announced it was time to head back and listen to the Test match between Australia and the West Indies from the MCG. Mum wasn't home yet, so we collected Alison and Christine on the way back. Dad lay on his bed with the radio nearby. I told him not to forget to remove his clothes, and he replied, chuckling, 'If I forget, I will wake up formal.' It was always one of his little jokes, along with the one of him having a bath just as the clock passed midnight on New Year's Eve, so he could tell everyone else they had not had a bath since last year. Dale and I moved to the adjoining room but could still hear the radio through the cardboard partition. Soon Dad was asleep, still in his clothes, and my brother and I quickly drifted off.

Suddenly, I was awoken by a bang from the front bedroom. Dad had fallen off the bed and was asleep on the floor. I tried raising him, but he kept muttering and refusing to move. Knowing he was drunk, I decided to leave him on the floor.

Moments later, another bang. This time it was Mum returning from the party. I went to greet her and told her about Dad. She, too, put it down to too much drink and said she'd get him back into bed. I heard her go to him to try to rouse him. There was no movement or muttering this time. Mum tried shaking and hitting him, but still no movement. 'Ricky, Ricky,' she yelled. She was becoming more frantic now, 'I don't think he's breathing. Go and get help.' Scared, I looked outside and screamed at a passing neighbour to come and help. She ran to Dad and removed her glasses, putting them under his nose, hoping to see some condensation. Nothing.

'I think he is dead,' she said.

Everyone started crying, and we all hugged. Mum kept repeating she knew this would happen and cursed his drinking. Finally, someone called for an ambulance as people gathered outside. The ambulance crew pronounced him dead but said they could not move him until the police arrived. That took a further two hours, and by then, the whole village was standing outside. I told the police what had happened, and the ambulance took the body away.

Left alone, we all burst into tears again and were grateful to cousin Norma for coming down from her home in Bathsheba to console Mum and take charge of affairs. The next day I telephoned Mr Duff and told him the bad news. He was very kind and told me there was no hurry to return, although Mum insisted I go back on my scheduled date of 13 January.

The burial was set for Wednesday, 31 December, at the St. Thomas parish church. In the days leading up to the funeral, Mum pulled herself together. She went to the coroner's inquest, which said he died from a cardiac arrest probably brought on by excessive alcohol. Unfortunately, her beloved Everson hadn't heeded the doctor's advice and sadly paid the price. The villagers were in as much shock as we all were. Only hours before his death, Dad had promised to be at my first Test match. He was full of life that evening and enjoyed having his eldest son at home. On the day of the funeral, you could feel the grieving all over the village. Dad had died in the same house he'd been born in back in 1937. The church was packed for the service, with many more outside.

Norma made refreshments at the house for everyone who wanted to return and offer their condolences. This was one New Year's Eve when no one felt like celebrating, and everyone drifted away long before midnight.

The next few days seemed to drag, and the house was empty without Dad. It was like he'd gone off to Pearl's shop but would never return. As the weekend approached, I began to pack my bags ready for England but also made time for Joyce, knowing it may be the last time I would see her for three months. She'd taken a day off and left Duana with her sister so we could be together. We talked, laughed, and cried until it was time to say goodbye, with me promising to ring before I left. I was concerned about leaving Mum so soon after losing Dad, but she insisted I return.

On Saturday morning after breakfast, I went around the village saying goodbye to all my friends. Check-in was 6pm, and my flight was due to depart two hours later. Norma's husband kindly agreed to take everyone to the airport in his van. Just before everyone bundled inside, I tried to call Joyce, but there was no answer. I made everyone wait while I tried repeatedly but there was no answer. It was all very subdued inside the van, remembering what it was like last time, with Dad, the chatter and the music. My thoughts drifted to Joyce. She knew I was going to call; where could she be? I was also concerned about Mum; how would she cope? How would she manage on one salary with all the household bills to take care of?

The airport came into view. My cases were off-loaded and taken to the desk, and then I turned to see Joyce standing beside her daughter. She had decided to come and see me off in person. I introduced her to mum before my flight was called, and I began my goodbyes and comforted Mum. They called the flight again, and tears began to flow as I whispered, 'I love you' to Joyce. I kissed her and Mum before proceeding through passport control without looking back, as I knew I'd break down and not want to leave. At the top of the steps, I did look back at the balcony and could just about make out the shapes of those waving. I waved back. After storing my bag in the overhead locker, I slumped into my seat, howling. This had been the most stressful time of my life, and it was a huge relief to let my emotions pour out.

It was around 7am when I arrived at Gatwick; I followed the other passengers through immigration and into the baggage hall. Then it was off to find Mr Duff, who had promised to be there for me. I couldn't find him, but soon became aware of an announcement, 'Would Ricardo Ellcock please contact the information desk.' Looking around, I followed signs towards the information desk and gave my name. A lady handed over an envelope. It contained a note from Mr Duff asking me to phone him and reverse the charges. The lady showed me to the telephone, and I made the call.

Mr Duff answered with his chuckle, 'Ricardo, we have had a blizzard here in Malvern, so I could not get down to Gatwick… how much money do you have?'

'Twenty pounds.' It was the money I'd had from when I'd left England and I hadn't changed it.

He chuckled again, 'Good, good, I want you to follow the signs to the train station and catch a train to Victoria. When you get there, I want you to call me again, and I will give you the rest of your initiative test.'

My trolley was overflowing, but I managed to negotiate a warren of corridors, escalators, and stairs until I reached a platform. A train was waiting, so I grabbed all my bags and jumped on just before the doors closed. I then realised, foolishly, I had no idea if it were the correct train, so I plucked up the courage to ask the smartly dressed man I'd sat beside. Thankfully, he confirmed we were heading for Victoria.

It was only a short journey, and I was soon trying to navigate the enormous station when a guard confronted me.

In what sounded like a Barbadian accent, he asked, 'Can I see your ticket, please?'

In my rush, I'd forgotten to buy one and immediately panicked.

'Where have you come from?' asked the guard once I'd admitted my error.

'Barbados, sir.'

The guard laughed, 'No, I mean which train station.'

I explained all about getting on at Gatwick and was asked for £2.80 before the guard began chatting about Barbados. He was from St. Andrew and had lived in England for 20 years; He showed me to the telephone boxes.

This time Mr Duff asked me to take a taxi to Paddington Station and ring him again.

'Well done, Ricardo. Now buy a ticket to Great Malvern. A train leaves at 1.35pm,' said Mr Duff, after I'd telephoned him for the third time in the morning.

I felt very relieved; soon, I would be on the last leg of the journey. It had been a tiring few hours. However, at the cashier's window, I was two pounds short of the ticket price. I couldn't believe it and didn't know what to do except walk away with tears streaming down my face. Perhaps I could beg for the extra two pounds; people were always kind to each other, weren't they? On that particular afternoon, everyone kept walking and ignoring my sorrowful pleas.

Then I saw a black guard standing proudly there in his uniform. Surely, he would come to my aid, I thought.

'I haven't enough money for my fare,' I told him. 'Can you give me two pounds, please, sir? The guard shook his head emphatically and aggressively said, 'No. And you are not supposed to beg in the station.'

My only option was to telephone Mr Duff again and tell him I hadn't enough money to get the train. He said, 'You had more than enough at Gatwick; what have you done with it?' His tone was so stern. All I could say was, 'Nothing, I have only paid for the train and the taxi.' He asked me how much the taxi was and when I told him he said eight pounds was absolutely outrageous.

'Was it a London taxi?'

'Yes,' I said.

'What colour was it, Ricardo?' asked Mr Duff.

'A brown Cortina.'

'That's not a London taxi. They are the black ones. That taxi driver has over-charged you.'

Mr Duff asked me to call him back in a few minutes whilst he made a few enquiries. When I did, he told me to sit tight, keep warm and wait for a couple of hours. Another boy, Simon Creffield, was also due to return to Malvern but was catching a later train and hadn't left his home in Essex. So, he would be bringing the extra money.

It was a long afternoon but Simon eventually arrived and I could buy my ticket and board the 5.05pm train. Cold, tired, and hungry, it wasn't long before I collapsed into a deep sleep, only waking once we reached Great Malvern station.

There was lots of snow around as Mr Duff greeted us. Back at school, it was nice to be warm again and enjoy Mrs Duff's excellent supper. I was allowed to phone Mum to tell her I'd arrived safely and then began unpacking and returning to Malvern life.

I couldn't help but reflect on how many changes had occurred in my life in the short time I'd been away. I buried myself in my schoolwork for much of the new term, and with cricket practice on Wednesday evenings, the occasional football game and various indoor activities, I was contented. However, that term's sport was rugby and I wasn't interested in that. Mr Duff wasn't happy at this and called me into his study and offered me an option. Either I played rugby, or I would have to do chores, called 'dirty jobs' for an hour, whilst the other boys were on the sports field. Presumably, he thought I'd back down and take the rugby option, but I didn't and spent the time cleaning up around the house, sweeping the dining room floor or laying the tables for the following morning's breakfast. Each of these tasks I found enjoyable, and began to look forward more and more to my hour of 'dirty jobs' as a little bit of 'me' time. I continued to write letters to Mum and Joyce but learnt an embarrassing lesson when I showed the others a letter Joyce had sent. She had put a lipstick kiss on the envelope, which caused much laughter and merriment. I decided my private letters would be kept private from then on.

One Saturday afternoon, my sponsor, Mr Clarke, and his girlfriend, Sandy, met me at Mrs Hunt's tea shop in Malvern Link. I enjoyed relaxing and listening to stories of Mr Clarke's time at Malvern, particularly the food. It seems all he was ever given was boiled cabbage; I was pleased the meals were more appetising nowadays. Whenever I met them, they brought me a few provisions and on this occasion there was a supply of cakes, fruit, biscuits, coffee, and orange squash. Mr Clarke told me how proud he was of me and said he was pleased he had invested in my future and hoped I would now step up for my family and play a bigger role since my father had died.

The weeks passed, and whilst I was very much looking forward to the cricket season, I was also looking forward to the Easter holidays when I could fly home. Shortly before the end of term, Mum wrote a letter asking if I could telephone an old friend of Dad's who lived in Harrow. Ranny worked with Dad as a foreign labourer in America before leaving Barbados in May 1965 to work on the London buses. He knew that Mum had been pregnant but had never met me. Mum had bumped into his brother in Bridgetown and had taken Ranny's telephone number. Armed with 10 pence pieces, I called the number, and a man with a strong Barbadian accent answered. I explained who I was and passed on the news about Dad. When my coins ran out, Ranny kindly called me straight back, asking more and more questions about me, the family and life back home. Mentioning I was returning to Barbados in a couple of weeks, he suggested I come and stay before the flight.

The final two weeks of term were spent working on my history project, 'The Atlantic Slave Trade,' and preparing for my trip home. This time it would be on a Sunday from Gatwick, on Caribbean Airways. Mr Duff spoke with Ranny and was happy for me to stay there. Arrangements were put in place for a meeting point outside Paddington station. Gary, Tony, and Neil would be on another coach, so I enjoyed my own company and looked at the beautiful scenery as we made our way to London. I took my bags and wondered where to go when I felt a tap on my shoulder. It was Ranny, who said, 'I knew it was you; you stand just like your Dad.' During the drive to his house, he pointed out one or two famous landmarks, then turned into Malvern Road – what a coincidence!

Ranny introduced me to his wife, Pearlene, and son, Mark, before a typically Barbadian meal of coucou and salt fish. Pearlene had even made real lemonade; it was like a home away from home. The conversation turned to Barbados and my dad; Ranny even had some old photographs of them together in America. Having spent a lovely evening in their company, I slept well and rose to find the others up and busy.

My flight wasn't until Sunday, so I was happy to accept Mark's offer to accompany him into the city. He was going to Oxford Street, somewhere I'd heard of but hadn't visited. We walked the short journey to Rayners Lane underground station; I was excited and thought this would be something else I could tell Mum. As we boarded the train, I thought it was pretty much like the one that had taken me back to Malvern in January, but within seconds we were plunged into a tunnel of darkness, and my ears popped.

Oxford Street was huge, with so many people milling around, nothing like Bridgetown. I saw a sign that said Tottenham Court Road and wondered if we were near the football stadium. Soon after arriving at Malvern, I'd become a Tottenham supporter after watching them beat Manchester City in the FA Cup Final on television. After browsing several shops, it was time to head back and sample more of Pearlene's excellent cooking. Ranny sat and checked the football pools, something I remember Dad doing. He'd had one or two small wins in his time and was always planning his exploits with the jackpot he was bound to win.

Ranny had promised Mr Duff he would deliver me personally to the check-in desk at the airport but felt his old Vauxhall wouldn't make it to Gatwick, so he decided to go with me on the train. Passing through Victoria, I looked at some of the taxis to see if I could see the driver who had overcharged me. We arrived at the check-in desk in good time, but there was a problem. I'd taken all my cricket kit home, hoping to get a game. The check-in lady said my cases were too heavy and I would have to pay an excess of £49. Explaining that I was a cricketer cut no ice. Caribbean Airways had no check-in staff on site, and the lady from Air Canada had never heard of cricket. She was adamant that my options were to pay the excess, take some stuff out, or miss the flight.

I asked if a Caribbean Airways representative was available to speak to me. There was, but I would have to stand aside as she had other passengers to process. Eventually, a young lady appeared and was very sympathetic to my situation. She seemed impressed when I told her I was a Worcestershire cricket player. She asked the check-in clerk to waive any fees. Ranny bought me a coffee and gave me a letter for Mum before it was time to thank him and head off to the departure gate. Without a window seat, I spent the first part of the flight working on my history project.

Thoughts soon turned to what lay ahead. Dad wouldn't be there this time. I remembered how happy he was to see me at Christmas and his line that he was 'going to drink from wine to iodine.' He probably overdid the drinking because I was back, and now he was gone forever.

How would Mum react to having me back, and would Joyce be as happy to see me as she was at Christmas? All of this was going through my head when the captain informed us we were beginning our descent into Bridgetown. We would be landing at 5pm, and the temperature was 82 degrees.

As the aircraft doors opened, I collected my bags from the overhead locker and followed the queue out through the front door. Stepping out onto the steps, I half expected Dad to be standing at the bottom. Following the other passengers into passport control, I looked up and saw a big glass window and there, waving frantically, I saw Mum, Norma, Dale, Alison, and Christine. I thought maybe Joyce was working and couldn't make it, but then Mum pointed further along the window and I saw her, full of smiles, also waving. Everyone came to kiss and hug me although Joyce whispered that she was shy, and we'd save our kiss until we were alone. Instead of a minibus, everyone had come to the airport in two cars, so I jumped into the back of one of them alongside Joyce. We held hands all the way back and made plans to catch up the next day, as Norma was going to take her home after I'd been dropped off.

The house felt very different this time as I stepped inside. Clearly, things would not be the same, although that could all wait for now.

Firstly, I had a lot of catching up to do with Mum.

CHAPTER 11

BECOMING A PEAR

The Easter break flew by, with my days spent between visits to Joyce, catching up with old friends and spending as much time as I could with Mum. I played cricket on weekends and squeezed in a visit to Combermere, causing quite a stir with many of my mates wanting to know all about England and playing cricket for Worcestershire. Although Mum might have had reservations about my relationship, she admitted she would rather I spend time with Joyce than be out on the streets. There'd been quite a few issues with teenagers being caught in possession of cannabis, with one or two houses in the village being raided by the police. Mum was extremely worried Dale would be caught up in it. She also reminded me I'd be doing my 'O' levels the following school term and told me to do my best, as she'd be praying for me.

I was bold enough to go and spend an entire night at Joyce's, and it was the best night ever, but we both knew it would be a long time before we could be together permanently. The following school holidays would coincide with the cricket season in England, so it might be Christmas before I'd see her again. Leaving everyone behind wouldn't be easy, but they all came to the airport to wave me off and wish me well. There were lots of tears as I hugged and kissed everyone.

Gary and Andrew had spent the holidays together and were already in the study when I got back to Malvern. There was also a surprise addition to the room, with a mini television on the table. I presumed it was Mr Duff's, but Andrew took ownership of it and said he would hide it until the start of the World Cup in Spain a few weeks later.

The weather was very mild for late April, so there was lots of opportunity to get on the cricket field. Coupled with my schoolwork, I found the routine enjoyable. My history project was eventually completed, and my marks improved in other subjects.

Cricket was creating an issue, however. I was taking lots of wickets for the first XI, but it was causing a lot of bad feeling among the other schools. They said my bowling was too fast and dangerous for that level, and some parents refused to let their children play against Malvern. It all came to a head in a match at Repton after they had won the toss and opted to bat first. I picked up a couple of early wickets, but one batter (I later discovered it was none other John Carr, who became a team-mate of mine at Middlesex), who was going along quite nicely until he tried to hook a bouncer and was hit flush on the head. He went down, falling on his stumps and was in some distress. He eventually had to be carried off the field.

The Repton master in charge of cricket felt it was unfair bowling and took his players off the field and threatened Repton would never play against Malvern again in any sport. The headmasters of both schools were called to speak to each other on the phone, but they could not resolve the situation, so Mr Duff was called from umpiring an under 14 game. After a lengthy discussion, he persuaded the Repton master to carry on with the game. Malvern took the field with an uneasy tension hanging in the air and dark clouds starting to build. No sooner had we returned to the field than the heavens opened, and very soon Repton's ground was under water and the game was called off. It was a miserable coach journey back to Malvern; I thought all public schools were against me and wondered if I'd be allowed to play again. Mr Duff was awaiting my return, and I was expecting bad news, but instead, he looked happy to see me.

'Ricardo, Ricardo, don't worry about today; I've got some great news for you,' he said. 'Worcestershire have offered you another summer contract.'

Overjoyed, I put Repton and their stupid cricket master out of my mind (although I did hope the batter I'd hit wasn't too badly injured!).

My summer cricket guaranteed, I could focus on my studies and worked harder and harder as 'O' level time drew nearer. I was sitting Maths, English Language, English Literature, History, Religious Studies, Physics, Biology, and Chemistry. The exams coincided with the start of the World Cup, so out came Andrew's little television and Gary and I joined him for the games. Word got around and a steady swell of boys came and joined us, with someone always on the lookout for Mr Duff.

On the evening England played their first match; it seemed like the whole school was crowded around watching. I took the first

Me as a four year old at Mum and Dad's wedding; passport photo of Dad; school days at Combermere (in the middle is Henderson Springer, former Barbados player and West Indies coach, now director of Barbados Cricket. Next to him is Adrian Armstrong, brother of former Barbados and Glamorgan fast bowler Gregory Armstrong).

Middlesex's four West Indian-born players who represented England, clockwise from top left; me, Roland Butcher, Norman Cowans and Neil Williams (RIP).

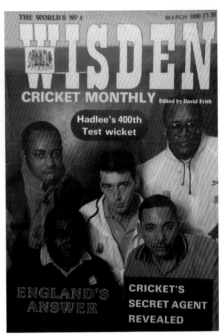

The cover of the *Cricketer* features England's four West Indies-born pacemen selected for the 1989-90 tour of the Caribbean in me, Devon Malcolm, Gladstone Small (another former Combermerian) and Phillip DeFreitas; *Wisden Cricket Monthly* adds Angus Fraser to show the complete pace attack; the full 1989-90 squad, with Chris Lewis (inset), another West Indies-born quick, who replaced me after my injury.

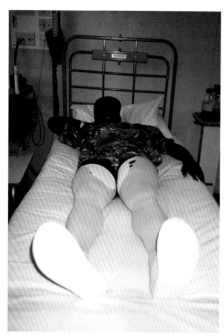
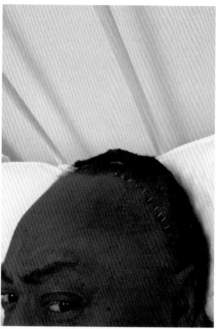

A couple of weeks after my first spinal operation at the Nuffield Hospital in Hove; the scars on my head after one of four brain operations at St Mary's Hospital in December and January 2018-2019; chatting with Middlesex teammates Angus Fraser, Norman Cowans, and Desmond Haynes, and Hampshire and West Indian great Malcolm Marshall (RIP).

In command of a 747-400 Jumbo; Macolm Marshall leads the conga; running a 10K in London after my brain operations.

Excited to meet Richard Roundtree (RIP), who played Shaft, on my flight; getting married to Kate on 1 October 1994 with cricketing colleagues and friends.

A Mercedes 300SL Convertible won in a John Player Special draw; a promotional photo for the 1990 tour; giving it everything.

Built for speed.

turn on the lookout, but as England scored early on, I couldn't resist going across to see the replay. As I did so, a familiar chuckle could be heard behind me.

'What have we got here?' he asked. 'You've all got exams coming up and should be working.'

The television had been switched off, and a cloth was thrown over it, so I wondered if he had even noticed it.

'Oh yes, I'll take this as well.' Of course he had!

He pointed at Gary, Andrew, and myself and told us he wanted to see us in his study after hall. Our punishment was to be 'gated' for three weeks, meaning we could go as far as the tuck shop but couldn't leave the school grounds. I looked for the positives and thought it would help me focus on my schoolwork, Andrew thought it was all a big joke, and Gary burst into tears as he'd never been in trouble before.

My first 'O' level exam was English Language, and as I walked into the exam room in the main college, my heart was beating faster and faster. When the bell went, the other boys began writing straight away. It distracted me, and I looked around, watching some of them. I thought I did OK and finished in good time before remembering something my dad had said before my Common Entrance Exam in Barbados: 'Always look over your work, cross your t's and dot your i's.'

The other exams came and went, some I found easier than others, with Physics and Biology being complete disasters. English Literature was all about Shakespeare's *A Merchant of Venice*, and even though I'd listened to the audiobook, watched the video, and seen it on stage, I still didn't understand it. But, on the other hand, Maths, History, and Religious Studies weren't as bad as I'd feared.

With schoolwork out of the way, I could relax and enjoy my cricket, taking lots of wickets. We hadn't lost a match all term and continued that sequence by winning the annual school festival in Shrewsbury. The organisers accommodated us in various boarding houses; the competing teams were ourselves, Rugby, Charterhouse, and Shrewsbury. I picked up 15 wickets across the three matches, and I was delighted for Neil MacLaurin, who made his debut and scored a very good 50 against Charterhouse. The end of term was quite a joyous occasion, our exams were out of the way, and we could spend time with some of the girls from the local schools. Playing and meeting up with the Worcestershire boys again was never far from my mind, and I had a chance to catch up when they played against the college. Soon it was time to join them regularly as Mr Duff dropped me off at Miss Collins' house for the summer. It was lovely to see her again, Popsy less so.

I was quickly back into the routine, with the club expecting me back in for training. I caught an early bus to the County Ground and was among the first to arrive. The coach greeted me warmly and revealed it was the plan for me to play in all of the second XI matches up until the end of the season and that I had been registered at Lord's as a Worcestershire player. However, I knew it was still very unlikely I would be playing any first XI matches any time soon.

The rest of the morning was spent practising with the first team, catching up with David, and hearing about his winter in Perth, Australia. At about 2pm, the session finished, and we piled into the dining room for sandwiches and soup. After an afternoon of fielding drills, it was time to call it a day and head with the others to the Shakespeare. The MG was still going, and David happily drove it as fast as ever. Drinks in the pub were followed by a nip along Main Street to get some Kentucky Fried Chicken before I decided to head back, leaving the others planning a visit to a nightclub. I had cricket for Worcester City the following day. Miss Collins was waiting with a message that I would be picked up by John Elliott, a Worcestershire committee member and wealthy local businessman, at 11.30am. The match was being played at West Bromwich Dartmouth, and with Worcester City third in the league, it was an important game.

John arrived to collect me in a shiny Mercedes 450 SL, and we chatted all the way there. The weather was gorgeous, and I enjoyed having the sun on my back as I knocked over the first three batters for hardly any runs. The opposition couldn't recover, and we bowled them out for 120, with me claiming 6-25 to set up an easy victory. I'd hoped for a match the next day but had been instructed to report in as Worcestershire were playing Middlesex in a Sunday League contest. Before the match, I was made to bowl to the first team and was a little surprised to see so many spectators around the practice area. Quickly shrugging off any nerves, I enjoyed the atmosphere and thrived on the encouragement the fans were giving. The match was so exciting, and I longed to be involved, but I had my list of chores, mixing drinks for the players when they were dismissed or for the thirsty fielders. The coach had promised I would feature in every game, and I kept putting pressure on myself to do well; I was so keen to give myself an opportunity to earn a full-time contract.

One match brought me down to earth, away against Ross-on-Wye, a beautiful little town but a boring cricket pitch with a flat wicket that didn't help me at all. I felt I should be getting more wickets than I was and prayed at night for some divine intervention.

So engrossed was I in the cricket, I'd almost forgotten about Malvern until Miss Collins handed me the phone one evening. It was Mr Duff. With a chuckle, he told me I'd passed several 'O' levels, including English Literature. I hadn't expected to pass that but was disappointed not to pass Maths and English Language. Physis was the disaster I expected. 'Never mind,' he told me, 'You can do your re-sits in November.'

During August, my luck changed a little on the field, and I picked up figures of 5-50 and 3-45 in a match against Somerset. This meant we went into the last match against Warwickshire at Shirley needing a win to lift the second XI championship. Shirley was a beautiful little ground on the outskirts of Birmingham. The ground was lush green but sloped slowly away to one side. The wicket was extremely brown and very hard. I went and had a prod at the pitch; it was the closest I'd seen to a Barbadian pitch. Bat all day, I thought!

A larger than usual crowd had turned up as it was a local derby, and Worcestershire v Warwickshire matches were always hot-blooded affairs with an atmosphere all of their own. The captain, Mark Scott, canvassed everyone's opinion on whether we should bat or bowl first. The dressing room was split fairly evenly, although I was strongly on the side of batting first. If there'd been more grass on it, then yes, have a bowl, but I'd seen enough wickets like this in Barbados, and you always wanted to bat first on them. Mark went out for the toss and returned to tell us he'd won it, and we would be bowling. I couldn't believe it. He had decided to field first on a wicket without a blade of grass, and the team needed to win the match to win the Championship. Surely the wicket would crack up, and the ball would be unplayable on the last day when we are batting. All these thoughts were rushing through my head as I got myself ready. 'First over, Ricky,' said Mark. I could barely look at him, thinking he'd gone completely mad.

Trying to create a positive mindset, I knew I'd have to take some early wickets before the shine and hardness came off the ball. It might become a little more challenging later. As I walked to the top of my run, I noticed Mr Clarke and Sandy sitting on a bench. They hadn't told me they were coming, but it was nice to see them. I ran in and decided to bowl a bouncer first ball to see what would happen. It sailed high over both the batter and wicket-keeper Peter Moores, future coach of Sussex, Notts and England, dropping about five yards inside the rope before crashing into the sightscreen. I didn't know I could bowl that fast! So, imagine what it did to the opposition! Both openers were quickly dispatched, and by lunch, I'd taken four wickets to leave Warwickshire on 50 for five, effectively 50 for six, as another player had gone to hospital with a broken arm. After lunch, I was brought back to the bowl to the lower order and whipped the hosts out for just 121, with me taking 7-46. Mr Clarke came over and congratulated me later, saying he had been to several matches without me knowing and was so proud of me, calling me the 'son he'd never had'.

That night I stayed in the hotel and resisted the temptation to go out with some of the others. Also, I knew we hadn't won yet, and this meant a lot to me. We built up a first-innings lead of around 160, and things looked good for us as I again got amongst the wickets, but the home side fought hard and cleared their deficit. I finished with 4-96, getting ten wickets in a match for the first time. To claim the title, Worcestershire had to score 96, and after the early loss of our captain, we raced to a nine-wicket triumph, the county's first silverware for a decade. It was a joyous dressing room, and the champagne flowed all the way back to Worcester and then to the Pavilion nightclub. I assumed this would be the end of my playing season and had been quietly tipped off I would be offered terms to return to the county in 1983. More than a few people had mentioned it, and there was a growing feeling the county was considering blooding some of their youngsters going forward. I sincerely hoped that included me.

For now, though, my thoughts drifted back to my studies and how I would improve my Maths and English Language, the two most important subjects. Physics was impossible, so less of a worry. Getting some quiet time to concentrate would be easier as I'd been made a prefect and given a bedroom to myself. I was sitting on the bed reading when Mr Duff found me. He was clearly excited about something.

'Worcestershire have rung and asked if you are available for selection for the first team tomorrow.'

I could scarcely believe it. Arrangements were put in place for me to be picked up at 9.30am the following morning, but I would have to attend the first lesson and travel in school uniform. The head also stipulated that I'd have to return to School House each night.

Leaving for the match, word had spread around the school, and several people were waiting to wave me off. Tim Curtis, the club's opening bat, had come to collect me in his blue Baby Austin, which sounded as if the suspension was about to drop off. As we drew closer to the County Ground, I remembered not knowing who we would be playing.

'Middlesex,' said Tim, 'And they only need eight points to win the County Championship!'

We drove into the car park, and I noticed someone getting his kit out of the boot of a Volvo. It was the Middlesex and former England captain Mike Brearley. It dawned on me nobody had confirmed I would be in the starting XI for this match. After all, I was only just 17 and knew I still had a lot to learn. Until anyone told me any different, I thought it best to head straight up to the second XI dressing room without realising how much of a stir my arrival would cause. No one at the club had seen me in my school uniform before, and seeing me in a plaid blazer with leather elbows, a blue shirt, grey trousers and a multi-coloured tie was clearly the funniest thing many of them had ever seen. David was on the floor, crying with laughter and muttering something about 'jazz hats', but I ignored him and quickly got changed to join the others for the warm-up.

As soon as I went downstairs, captain Phil Neale, came over and confirmed I was playing, but he added I'd got plenty of time to prepare because Middlesex had won the toss and decided to field. His words filled me with so much joy. I had been selected for my first-class debut!

Worcestershire were soon in trouble, and as the day wore on, I grew increasingly nervous, awaiting my turn to bat. Eventually, I walked out as last man to a polite ripple of applause but, sadly, I didn't delay anyone for too long, given out lbw for nought against the England spin bowler, John Emburey. We'd only made 168, and the skipper was clearly hoping for me to make an immediate impact. As I removed my pads, he said I would be opening from the Diglis End. 'What?' I asked, not knowing the proper name for the scoreboard end. I noticed my sweaty palms and hoped the ball wouldn't slip out. The captain gathered the team around, 'Right boys, let's give it our best shot and chase everything. Good Luck. Ricky, you bowl first ball.' Middlesex had a powerful batting line-up, with former England captain Mike Brearley opening with another player destined for Test cricket, Wilf Slack. Brearley was on strike for the first ball, but as I started to run in, I felt the ball slipping, so I stopped and wiped my hand on the grass. Our captain offered gentle encouragement, and I ran in for a second time, bowling a ball outside the off stump, which Brearley let go. My team-mates were supportive, getting behind me at every opportunity, and my confidence was lifted by an opening maiden. I felt my first spell was pretty good, although I didn't have a wicket to show for it and by the end of the day, Middlesex had eased past our total, and I was still wicketless. I showered and put my uniform back on and Tim gave me a lift back to Malvern. As county debuts go, my first day ended differently than most others, with my head stuck firmly inside a textbook.

The match resumed on the Monday, and I justified my selection by taking three wickets. After having Phil Edmonds caught for 92, I dismissed Simon Hughes and Norman Cowans to finish with the respectable figures of 3-80 and the distinction of hitting the former England captain on the head. By this stage, Middlesex had secured their fourth batting bonus point to add to the four they had collected for bowling. The eight points were all they required to be crowned county champions of England. I still felt I had something to offer as I walked out to bat for a second time, determined not to make another nought. After taking guard from umpire Roy Palmer, I settled down to face the Middlesex fast bowler Simon Hughes. The first ball whooshed past. I hardly saw it and was fortunate it was wide of the stumps. The same happened with the next delivery, but then I snicked the third, and it raced away through the slips for four. After that, I felt better and was 13 not out at the end of our innings. We'd only left Middlesex a modest target to chase, and they cantered to a 10-wicket victory on the final day. Completely exhausted, I sat in the home dressing room as the celebrations went on next door. I drew confidence from the encouraging comments from team-mates and supporters and knew I could cut the mustard at this level. 'Whatever happens now,' I thought, 'I'm a county cricketer.' The only downside was that it was the end of the season, and I'd have such a long wait before I could enjoy the experience again.

Back at Malvern, it seemed as if I'd become a celebrity overnight, the masters asking me about the experience and telling me the school had not had a serving pupil play first-class cricket before. The news also hit Barbados, with Mum calling me before I could ring her. She told me how proud the whole village was, and we both said we wished Dad had still been alive to share the moment. I could imagine him announcing to everyone, 'The drinks are on me!'

What I most cherished was the opportunity to continue my cricket career, which became possible when Worcestershire sent through a full-time contract for the 1983 season... Once I'd re-taken my exams, my days at Malvern were over.

Plans were already set for me to return to Barbados early, and I would be back in time to play in the Barbados first-division competition. Saying goodbye to everyone was hard, as I'd made some good friends at Malvern, mainly down to the kindness of Mr Clarke, Mr Duff, Mr Murtagh and the others. During my final assembly, the headmaster told the school I was leaving, and everyone clapped and seemed very excited for me.

Mr Clarke loaded all my kit into his Aston Martin for the journey to Heathrow. What an amazing time it had been since I'd first arrived in England! I promised him I was determined to make the most of the opportunity he'd given me. He had backed me, and so had Worcestershire.

Now, it was down to me to discover if I had the necessary attributes to make it as a county cricketer.

CHAPTER 12

REPRESENTATION

I registered for Carlton on my return to Barbados but only made one appearance before the season ended. I kept fit by practising and training with the Barbados under 19 side. The months drifted by, with my days split between time with Mum, the family and evenings with Joyce. Christmas was quite a low-key affair. As usual, there was plenty to eat, but not too many people were drinking alcohol, with the anniversary of Dad's death uppermost in our thoughts. We honoured him with his customary saying just after midnight on New Year's Eve, with everyone saying, 'You haven't had a bath since last year!'

During January, Mr Duff telephoned with great news; I'd somehow passed all my retakes, including physics; he joked about miracles and divine intervention. March eventually arrived, and it was time to head back to England; pleased to travel as a cricketer and not as a student for the first time. Arrangements had been made for me to return to Miss Collins. The flight went smoothly, and there was no hint of any issues until I arrived at passport control. A charming Scottish customs officer asked me the purpose of my visit to England there. I proudly explained I was here to play professional cricket. She asked how long I proposed to stay, and slightly aggrieved she didn't know the length of a cricket season, I said six months. Next, she asked to see my work permit. I didn't have one. I was denied entry and told I would be held until a flight was available to return me to Barbados. Panicking, I told her my guardian Mr Clarke was waiting for me outside. She took his name, but before I could say anything else, security led me to the cells. Soon a key was turned in the lock.

I was trapped, alone and scared.

I was left for what seemed like ages, with thoughts whirling through my mind. I began to cry and cry and cry. I shouted, but nobody came. Then I heard a key in the lock, and the door slowly opened. I assumed they must have found an aeroplane to fly me back to Barbados.

The immigration officer walked in.

'Good news, sir, we've found your work permit.'

My passport was stamped, and I was allowed into the country. Mr Clarke explained he'd telephoned Mr Vockins, the Worcestershire secretary, once he'd been made aware of the issue. Mr Vockins told him the work permit was already at Heathrow with the immigration department and this was all a 'huge cock-up'.

A Heathrow jail made me the talk of the dressing room as I became accustomed to pre-season training. There was a lot of physical exertion, with morning sessions spent running along the Severn and back for shuttles and exercises. Because it was often too wet outside, afternoons were spent bowling indoors at the Royal Grammar School, and the days lasted from 9.30am to 4.30pm, with a break for soup and sandwiches. This continued from 1 April until the day before the first match on 21 April.

I started the season in the first team and got a few wickets, but I found it all very tiring, and my performance began to slide off. I found myself alternating between the firsts and the seconds. One day Mr Vockins called me into his office. He explained he had received a letter from the Barbados Cricket Association asking if Worcestershire would consider releasing me for a short period to represent Barbados in the West Indies under 19s tournament. He said the club would have to agree at a committee meeting but wondered what my thoughts were. Naturally, I was over the moon! I'd always wanted to represent my country and had missed the two previous tournaments because I was away attending Malvern. The tournament was for four weeks in July and was being held in Jamaica; it was agreed I could attend before returning to finish the English season. Returning to Barbados meant a day at home before meeting the team the following day. I knew the others, having either played with or against them in the past.

Jamaica was in turmoil, with elections not too far away and daily reports of people being shot. Our accommodation was the Mico College, on the outskirts of downtown Kingston. Armed forces were out on the streets, and at night the silence was broken by sporadic machine gun fire. It was all pretty scary. Our team manager called a meeting about safety and asked us to remove any items of jewellery when out on the streets and to avoid wearing any bright red or blue clothing, the colours of the two political parties.

We started the tournament strongly, defeating Guyana by an innings and 20 runs in our opening match, played at the police headquarters ground in Kingston. Winning with a day to spare meant we had the somewhat dubious honour of being allowed to go shopping in downtown Kingston. I thought it was filthy, with several windows shot through. In contrast, we then looked around uptown Kingston, which was beautiful, with many new buildings and posh residences. They were only about two miles apart but looked like different countries.

The next match was three days later against the Leeward Islands, again at the police headquarters. We won easily, putting us through to the final. We spent a couple of days sightseeing and shopping for gifts while awaiting the outcome of the Jamaica v Trinidad match. Jamaica, the winners, travelled with us to the Alpart Ground in the Mandeville region, a hilly three-hour drive. A sizeable crowd was in attendance on the first morning, with it being around 90 degrees and not a cloud in sight. All the windows to the dressing room were opened to let in as much air as possible.

We batted first, scored 453 and immediately put Jamaica under pressure with a cluster of early wickets. Myself and Milton Small (who later played Test cricket for West Indies) were the two-leading wicket-takers in the tournament, we shared the workload as we went on to win the match (by an innings and 230 runs) and the championship. In the first innings of the final, I took 7-32, and Milton had identical figures in their second innings. Between us, we took 36 wickets across the three matches.

The newly crowned West Indies under 19 champions had a chirpy flight back to Bridgetown. I had 48 hours to enjoy the success before my return to England. Mr Vockins, met me at Heathrow and drove me back to New Road, where the first team were playing Somerset in a Sunday League match. Disappointingly, that was as close as I got to the first team in the final few weeks of the season. My second team performances weren't anything special. Still, I was not expecting to be frozen out of the first team picture, and it was a relief to find myself heading back to Barbados at the end of September. There was still time to get some cricket at home, and I made four appearances for Carlton before the end of the Barbados cricket season. My only first-class experience had been for Worcestershire, and I was eager to push myself for selection for the Barbados side. The chance to represent my home nation appealed, and I made myself available for the trials. The West Indies side was away in Australia, and many star names had gone on tour. This was also a period when several other likely replacements had been banned from the game for their part in a rebel tour to South Africa, so Barbados cricket was in a period of transition. However, the country had forged a reputation over many decades for producing some of the world's finest fast bowlers. The conveyor belt of quicks meant plenty of talented options would still be vying for places.

After Christmas, the names of the triallists for the Barbados Shell Shield side were announced, and I was included. During the trials, I felt I bowled well but didn't pick up many wickets, so I wondered if I'd done enough. It looked as if the competition for the fast-bowling places was between myself, Milton Small, Roddy Estwick and Neil Philips, who played their cricket in the Lancashire league.

The first match was to be played from 20-23 January against Trinidad & Tobago in Barbados. It was customary for the team to be announced on the radio a few days beforehand. When I was younger, I remember sitting with my dad listening to the announcements and then watching his reaction. I so wished he was there with me to share this moment. I listened to the radio all day, and eventually, at 7pm, the team was announced.

I had been included! Although I'd represented Barbados at under 19 level, to represent your country's senior team was a tremendous accolade. My thoughts were already wandering towards my next ambition and fulfilling my dream of playing Test cricket. Kensington Oval is the home of Barbados cricket. Although I'd been there many times as a spectator and for training, playing in front of family and friends and wearing the Barbados shirt was one of the most amazing experiences of my life. I picked up a wicket in my first spell, which settled me, and I got two more later on as we easily won by six wickets. The next match was also at home, against the Windward Islands, and we'd have beaten them if the rain hadn't washed out the final day. Carlisle Best, our captain, had scored a fine century to leave them a victory target of 324, and by the close of the third day, Milton and myself had removed both openers.

We then flew to St Kitts and Nevis to play against the Leeward Islands, and I was rested for this match, but watching Andy Roberts performing was a tremendous experience. The great West Indies fast bowler had recently retired from Test cricket but was still a force to be reckoned with. He took ten wickets in the drawn contest. We needed to beat Jamaica at Kensington to win the Shield, and the selectors stuck with the same XI. Disappointed not to feature, I was still overjoyed to see my team triumph, and I was more than happy to share in their success. I returned to the side as we finished the campaign against Guyana at the Bourda Ground, and then it was back to Bridgetown for the trophy presentation. To collect my Shell Shield winner's medal from Governor General Sir Hugh Springer, and having Mum and Joyce there to support me, was one of my proudest moments.

Although I'd felt fit and pain-free during those matches, after returning to Worcester for pre-season training, I started to feel irritation in my back. The weather wasn't great, so we'd been bowling on the indoor surfaces, and I wondered if that had been a factor. The coach sent me to be checked out by the physio 'Pinkie', who diagnosed a strained muscle at the top of my buttocks and advised rest. Frustratingly, I had to sit out the first few weeks of the season, restricting my physical exertions to a daily swim.

Everything appeared to have cleared up within two weeks, and I was selected for the first team. I took five wickets as we rolled Sussex in two days, but after a couple more outings, things started to take their toll, and I was again left out and told to rest up. Another request arrived from the Barbados Cricket Association asking if I could be released to play in the youth championships, but although the club were keen to back me if I wanted to go, I felt I needed to cement my place in the Worcestershire first team. My determination to nail down a permanent spot wasn't solely confined to fitness issues. The county had signed an up-and-coming and very talented young Zimbabwean batter by the name of Graeme Hick. The regulations limited each side to one overseas player per game, so it looked as if I would be sharing a spot with him, depending on the team's requirements.

Towards the end of the season, my back pain intensified once again. After seeing Dr Davies and being advised to rest, I spent two weeks in London with Ranny and Pearline before flying home. I again took part in the Barbados trials for the Shell Shield side. This time my vigil beside the radio wasn't rewarded, and I didn't make the XI to play in the first match against Guyana. Perhaps I'd misread the signals, but I felt sure I would be selected and couldn't take it in. It ate away at me for a few days. Poor Joyce seemed to take the blame for my disappointment. There appeared to be a permanent tension between us, and we argued for much of the time. My response was to go out, practise hard, and show the coaches I deserved to be picked. Someone must have noticed because I earned a recall for a one-day match against the Leeward Islands at Kensington. I got a wicket in my second over but could already feel the pain in my back. The smart thing to do would have been to let my team-mates and coaching staff know and leave the field, but I wondered if I'd ever be picked again if I did that. This was my chance to impress and nail down a starting spot in the team. I managed to get through my spell of six overs and came back to bowl a couple more later in the innings, but soon it was clear I couldn't carry on. I hadn't experienced pain like it before and returned to Redman's Village in absolute agony. My mum tried several remedies to ease my suffering – heated breadfruit leaves, candle grease, Epsom salts and hot water.

But nothing worked.

Despite our recent difficulties, I thought I'd let Joyce know I was in pain and staying with Mum, but when I rang her, I was shocked as a man answered the phone. Convinced she was having an affair, I slammed down the receiver and vowed our relationship was over.

The next day I telephoned the British Airways office and brought forward my return flight to the UK. For the first and only time, I didn't want to be in Barbados. Mr Clarke picked me up from the airport, and I stayed with him for a while before moving back to Worcester and my old room at Miss Collins. There was no respite from the back pain, and the club doctor said it was probably torn ligaments and recommended bed rest. We weren't getting anywhere with my issues, and the club was running out of patience. They felt I was faking an injury and didn't want to play, which couldn't have been further from the truth. They ordered me to turn out for the second team. I knew it was hopeless, but I tried my best, turning my arm over at a very gentle medium pace. No one helped, which made it worse, and I resorted to the self-help remedies of hot baths and Ralgex in desperation.

But, of course, nothing helped.

It was clear that the club would sack me at the end of the season. Miss Collins seemed to be the only one who knew my pain. My Saturdays had been spent playing for West Bromwich Dartmouth, and although second in the league, even they were frustrated. Fellow professional and former England test player David Steele was scoring lots of runs and taking lots of wickets with his left-arm spin. That only highlighted that I wasn't giving value for money, and club members weren't shy in telling me I hadn't pulled my weight and didn't look like I was trying.

On one particular day, West Brom won the toss and put the visitors, Stourbridge, into bat. I gradually increased my pace as I ran in to bowl. I yelped as I delivered my first ball. The pain was shooting down my legs, and I had pins and needles in my toes. I feared I would black out and told the captain I couldn't continue. I'd never experienced anything like it and had to suffer the humiliation of being booed from the ground by a small section of our supporters as I hobbled off. It was too much to take, and I burst into tears once I returned to the dressing room. My day could hardly have got any worse, but then the manager burst in shouting that he would be writing a strong letter of complaint to Worcestershire.

All I could do was sob and ask for someone to take me home.

I was eventually diagnosed with fractures of the spine – L3, 4 and 5 – and plastered from below my neck to just above my private parts.

Shortly afterwards, Worcestershire were playing in a Benson and Hedges cup semi-final at New Road, so I got a taxi down to support them. It was a baking hot day, and I couldn't get comfortable on the balcony with my plaster, so I took my shirt off and lay on the dressing room floor watching the match on television. Nobody – and I mean nobody – spoke to me.

Surely they could see I hadn't been faking the injury.

They didn't want me there, so I left them to it and got another taxi home. Gathering pen and paper, I sat and wrote to Mum, assuring her I would be feeling better soon. I thought about writing to Joyce but as I hadn't heard from her since I'd left Barbados. I didn't see the point. Too proud to write the first letter, I decided the relationship was properly over.

As the days went by, I became more accustomed to wearing the plaster and began to sleep better. David remained my one true friend; occasionally he'd come around, and we'd go for a drink. He knew about Joyce, of course, and told me about a friend of his I may be interested in getting to know. Her name was Moey; she was 28 and married with two kids. I followed David's suggestion, we met and got along exceptionally well. She was very kind and willing to listen to all my problems. We began to meet regularly for a drink and talked most days on the telephone. The more I saw of her, the more I liked her, and I could feel myself falling for her, although I wondered why she was happy to spend so much time with me whilst still married.

On 7 September, I headed to Birmingham for my follow-up appointment with my orthopaedic surgeon. I took a towel and some fresh soap to shower after the plaster was removed. Before I went in to see him, I did a little test of my own, squeezing the muscles in my back to try and see if there was any pain. There was no pain; I was sure it had healed, so I entered the room full of optimism.

The doctor poked at the plaster cast, 'It is a little soft in the front, so can you reinforce it and let him wear it for another six weeks.'

I was devastated and pleaded with him to let me have a shower, but he just uttered, 'No, you will be OK. I'll see you in six weeks.'

Six weeks, six weeks, why was everything six weeks? The drive back to the house seemed to take six weeks. When I got there, I slowly climbed the stairs and fell onto the bed, tears streaming down my face. Moey phoned later to ask if the plaster was off and tried her best to cheer me up when she heard how depressed I was. She asked if it would be OK to drive over and see me. I assured her Miss Collins was going to be out all evening.

When Moey arrived, we chatted for a while, and I was getting all sorts of signals I didn't know how to react to. Eventually, I just reached across and kissed her gently on the lips. She responded immediately; I could tell she was as keen as I was to take our relationship further. We struggled upstairs, plaster restricting my every move, and lay on the bed kissing and exploring each other's bodies. The cast made it difficult to manoeuvre, but she was eager to continue and managed to climb on top of me. Afterwards, she lay there, staring at the ceiling. I asked if she felt guilty about what had just happened. She said she didn't, but it didn't mean she would ever leave her husband. She wanted to be with him, for their children's sake.

As I continued my rehabilitation, I saw Moey occasionally but only for the odd drink or a chat, as she felt we should just be friends.

Eventually, on 18 October, I was cut free from my plaster cast. The news had been good. I was pain-free, and X-rays confirmed the cracks had healed properly. Left with the choice of what to do for the rest of the English winter, I decided against returning to the Caribbean. My period out of the game meant I wouldn't be considered for any of the Barbados matches, so I opted to get myself fit again and resume with Worcestershire in peak condition.

CHAPTER 13

A TASTE OF CHAMPAGNE

Because of the time I had spent in education at Malvern, under the regulations, I would become eligible to play for England by 1988 and set that as a new goal. I embarked on a programme of gym work and running, running, running. It all went so well for a couple of months that I popped back to Barbados to spend Christmas with Mum.

My village side roped me in to play a couple of matches for them, which I enjoyed, and without getting too strenuously involved, it reassured me I was getting back to full fitness. My training programme had been carefully planned out by Worcester. As the season neared, I was bowling faster and faster and was promised I would be very much in the mix when deciding on overseas players. Unfortunately, it didn't pan out that way. I was told the wicket wasn't suitable for each of the first few matches and was left out. My only match practice was for the seconds and West Bromwich on Saturdays.

However well I was doing, I knew I wouldn't play for the first team unless something happened to Graeme Hick. I'd heard the committee felt he should play in all of the matches, and to be fair he scored over 2,000 runs in the County Championship that year. My only first XI appearance that summer was in the tour match against India, and, typically, much of the contest was lost to the rain. So, it wasn't surprising I jumped when an opportunity came out of the blue to represent my old school. The Secretary of the Old Malvernians phoned and asked if I was interested in representing the OMs in the Cricketer Cup. Worcestershire wouldn't stand in my way, so I played through the qualifying rounds and helped them reach the final, staged at Vincent Square, the ground of Westminster School. It was a very grand affair, sponsored by both *The Cricketer* magazine and Moet & Chandon champagne. As befits such an occasion, there was lots to enjoy about the off-field activities, with plenty of multi-coloured blazers, straw hats and attendees enjoying the sponsors' food and drink, as well as laying out their travel rugs and picnics on the boundary edge.

113

Our opponents were Downside Old Boys from Somerset. We managed to bowl them out for 228, having elected to field. We ran into some early difficulties, but former England wicket-keeper Roger Tolchard and I combined to successfully chase down our target. It's always a nice feeling to play a part in helping your side to victory, especially when there is a liberal supply of complimentary champagne to celebrate. Apart from our medals, we learned a special prize was on offer. Later in the year, we would all be invited on a trip to Epernay in France for a visit to the Moet & Chandon château and cellars. Confined to the second XI for the remainder of the season, I was ready for a break as I headed to Gatwick for our flight to France on 4 October. It was good to catch up with the rest of the party as we assembled by the check-in desk. Everyone was in high spirits until I was asked for my ticket.

I couldn't find it anywhere!

Panicking, with a mixture of embarrassment and desperation, I began rifling through my bags in despair. Finally, after what seemed like an eternity, I think the lady on the desk felt sorry for me and said she'd cleared it with her bosses to issue me a replacement ticket. I couldn't thank her enough and only began to relax once we were airborne and drinking our first glass of complimentary fizz. This was my first visit to the continent. As we left Rheims Airport on our luxury coach, I was instantly fascinated by the spectacle of everyone driving on the 'wrong side of the road', something I had previously only witnessed from an aircraft window.

We did the full touristy bit, wandering around the vineyards and being shown how white juices were released from the red grapes. Then we went to the château, an enormous house in the middle of all the vines. It was a magnificent building, dripping in elegance and full of beautiful paintings. Despite the majestic surroundings, something else – or, rather, someone else – caught my eye as we sat down to lunch. A beautiful young lady. Our eyes met briefly. She smiled and then looked away quickly. While coffee was being served, I seized my moment, plucked up enough courage to move my chair closer to hers, and then introduced myself. She told me her name was Kate Toft, she worked for Moet & Chandon in London and had organised the day for us. She was stunning, and I couldn't keep my eyes off her for the rest of the day, but she didn't seem interested and moved quickly away each time I tried to speak to her.

As the day drew to a close and we headed back to the airport, I again tried my luck and asked her if I could have her telephone number. She refused, so I thought it wasn't meant to be. Over the weekend, I recalled she said she worked for Moet & Chandon in their London offices, so on the Monday morning, I tracked down the office number and asked to speak to Kate. Soon she was on the phone, and I asked if I could take her out when next in London. She said she was 'very busy' and 'probably' wouldn't be able to make it. Undeterred, I hatched a plan. I was running out of the money I'd saved during the season and thought I'd have to sign on the dole to keep myself going. Help was at hand from a friend – Ranny said it would be fine to stay with him if I came down for the weekend. I rang Kate back and told her I would be in London anyway and would like to see her on the Sunday if she wasn't too busy. She mentioned something about a prior engagement but asked for an address (Ranny's) and said she'd try to come around in the afternoon if she could get away.

That was all I heard – YES, she'd said YES!

The following Sunday afternoon was the most anxious I'd ever been, and to cap it all, Ranny's doorbell hardly stopped ringing. First, friends came round visiting, then Ranny's son arrived. Each time the doorbell went, I hoped it would be Kate.

By 3pm, I'd practically given up, but then another ring, and it was for me. She had come, after all. We drove to Hampstead and walked on the heath, chatting about the trip to the château, our jobs and our families. She was very easy to get along with, bright, intelligent and just a joy to be with. We were both hungry, so she suggested we head back to her place in Muswell Hill, which she shared with two other girls.

My plans were fairly flexible, but I intended to get a late train back to Worcester. Kate rang to find the train times but said I'd already missed the last train and offered me the use of her sofa-bed for the night. It had been a lovely evening, and I was more than happy to accept her kind offer. The following morning, as I watched her getting ready for work, I knew I'd fallen for her. She was the woman of my dreams. As soon as I got back to Worcester, I ordered some flowers to be sent to her,

'With love from a Mystery Man', I put.

Our relationship developed quickly from then on; we spoke daily on the phone and wrote plenty of letters. Prior to meeting Kate, I'd already made plans to return to Barbados for Christmas. We'd already discussed how being apart for almost three months would test what we felt for each other. Because of that, I had no hesitation in packing my bags early and heading back to London to spend a week with her before my flight. To say we got on is an understatement, and this time I didn't have to spend the nights alone on the sofa bed. It broke my heart to leave her, and we both shed a few tears when she dropped me off at the airport. Our time apart dragged, but we survived and she was there to greet me on my return.

During pre-season training, the committee dropped a bombshell on me. They had agreed a deal with Farsley Cricket Club in the Bradford League if I wasn't required for the first team. Neil Radford had joined from Lancashire in 1985 and taken 100 wickets in a season, Phil Newport had broken through into the first team, Paul Pridgeon was owed a benefit for his loyalty; and with Ian Botham and Graham Dilley joining in 1987, I was surplus to requirements. I could see what was happening. Worcester wanted me as far away from New Road as possible and had no interest in playing me. Former England captain Raymond Illingworth, the tamer of tear-away England quickie John Snow, skippered Farsley and was put in charge of my development. It meant a round trip of 300 miles every weekend. Kate and I found a compromise, although it meant lots of driving for us both. Her mum lived in Staffordshire, so we would meet there on Friday evenings and then travel to Yorkshire on Saturday mornings. Despite the miles involved, it meant we could spend every weekend together.

Farsley were enjoying a very successful season and made Kate and me feel very welcome. We entered into the spirit of things by attending all of their social events. One of them included a competition run by John Player Special cigarettes – one of the principal cricket sponsors in the UK. We'd spent so much time together by now that we decided to move in together during the off-season. Kate moved out of her shared accommodation and into her own place on a council estate in Peckham in south London. I had to return to Worcester every two weeks to sign on. On one of these return trips, I called into Miss Collins' to collect my mail and opened an envelope that said I'd won a major prize in a draw. I thought it was junk mail and wondered how they'd got my address. I did note it had John Player Special on the envelope, so I thought perhaps I'd won some cigarettes. I put it to one side and forgot about it.

A couple of weeks later, I made the same journey, and Miss Collins asked me to pick up some cigarettes for her on the way back from signing on. Head like a sieve, I had completely forgotten the prize envelope. I thought maybe I had won some cigarettes and could give them to Miss Collins, even though they were not her brand. The instructions were to call the marketing manager. He answered the phone, asked for my name, checked a few details, and said, 'Congratulations, Mr Ellcock, you have won a car in our promotion draw.'

I couldn't believe it!

'What kind of car is it,' I eventually asked.

'It's a Mercedes 300SL.'

'Shiiiiiiiiiiiii.........t.'

'No, it's not shit, sir. It's black.'

I decided to ask local businessman John Elliott to sell it on. On the Monday morning, as soon as he opened for business, he received an offer of £32,000 from someone in London, and a week later it was sold. The money was deposited into my bank account, with £1,000 sent to Mum, who needed to have some repair work done on the house. I put the rest to good use, buying a house overlooking the River Severn.

The 1988 season was going to be a big one for me because I was now qualified to play for England, which meant I could play for Worcestershire whether there was another overseas player or not. Sadly, my hopes and expectations weren't matched by the county. And despite doing well in the pre-season matches, I wasn't included for the first Championship match. It meant I was once again driving to Yorkshire.

The thought of continuing my career like this was depressing, and I decided to look for other opportunities. My winters had been spent in Barbados or England, and the prospect of going to either Australia or New Zealand was starting to appeal. On the notice board in the New Road dressing room, several clubs from those two countries were advertising for players. Encouraged by Dipak Patel, I wrote to his club side in Auckland and received an exciting offer. They would pay my airfare and $300NZ a week but wanted me to do some coaching around the local schools. This was a better proposition than staying behind and signing on the dole.

As the season drew to a close, I had become totally disheartened with Worcestershire. There was no chance of a game however well I'd been performing, and I knew a parting of ways was inevitable. However, they had been enjoying a terrific run of results and were top of the County Championship and through to the final of the NatWest Trophy. Soon enough the County Championship pennant returned to Worcestershire but as the champagne flowed, I was in tears. I knew my association with them was over. They didn't want me, and I didn't want to play for them again. I told the chairman I wanted to leave, and after a brief discussion, he agreed it was OK for me to look elsewhere.

Kate gave up her job to travel to New Zealand with me, but before we left I drove to Malvern to catch up with Mr Duff. He was very understanding about my position and said he'd help draft a statement to circulate to other clubs about my availability. By the time we were ready to leave on 25 September, Middlesex and Surrey had contacted me with offers. Mr Duff told me not to rush into things, to take my time and consider all options carefully.

Kate and I flew out of Gatwick on Continental Airlines Flight CO009 to Houston at the start of our adventure. I'd never been to the United States and was looking forward to the one-week break in Los Angeles before continuing our journey to Auckland. Although our relationship was pretty solid, we knew this could be a testing period because we would be living in each other's pockets for six months.

LAX airport was the very definition of chaos and confusion, and it was with some relief I hailed a taxi down and thanked the driver as he loaded our luggage into the boot.

'Where to?' he yelled.

'Airport Holiday Inn, please,' reading from a sheet containing all my travel details.

'Are you kidding me?' he bellowed. 'Shit man, don't you people know there is a fucking free bus to the Holiday Inn?' It was a two-minute drive!

He took us anyway and grabbed the five dollars before screaming off into the distance.

Beverly Hills was the most spectacular part of the journey, exactly how I imagined LA. The streets were very clean, and the grass verges immaculate. Our tour bus driver pointed out the homes of the rich and famous, including Madonna and Sean Penn, Sylvester Stallone, George Burns, Victoria Principal, and Barbara Streisand. All of the houses were huge and had electric gates. They were even bigger than the Richardsons, I thought.

The rest of the tour took in various scenic spots, like the Beverly Hills Hotel, which was pink, plus the beautiful Chinese theatre. Everywhere we went, we saw the most magnificent cars, from Ferraris to Mercedes, Rolls Royce to luxury limousines. During the rest of the week, we continued to explore. At Universal Studios, we saw the car from *Back to the Future* and screamed in delight as our tour bus was 'attacked' by both Jaws and King Kong. Then it was on to Disneyland, where the queues were horrendous. That caused a pointless argument; Kate was unwilling to wait for the rides. It was the first sign of growing tension between us. Kate's mother had warned her it might not work out as we were from such different backgrounds. She was from a white middle-class family, with her mum a doctor and her father a Russian teacher.

I was black and from a very poor family in Barbados.

But we saw no problems. We were in love and enjoying each other's company.

Sad at leaving such a beautiful place, we bid farewell to the USA. Continental Airlines Flight 002, LA to Honolulu and on to Auckland.

CHAPTER 14

IMPORTANT STEPS

The chairman and other club members were there to meet us at the airport, but I had to do a spot of cleaning before I could enter New Zealand. Inspecting my bags, a customs officer noticed some soil stuck to the studs of my cricket boots. So as not to bring any disease into New Zealand which could affect the sheep, I was made to stand and scrub my boots clean in front of the officer.

First impressions of a new country are significant. As we drove from the airport, Kate thought it was strange that there were so many wooden houses. It hadn't occurred to me, as the majority of the houses in Barbados are also made of wood. That aside, the scenery and the road design were very similar to England.

Birkenhead is on Auckland's north shore and is linked to the city by a bridge, a little like the Sydney Harbour Bridge in appearance. Water was everywhere, and the weather was distinctly chilly, which surprised me as I'd anticipated New Zealand would be warm all year around, like Barbados. Our accommodation was just across the road from the club chairman. It was a one-bedroom flat attached to the back of his parents' house. Originally, it had been built for his grandparents, but they had died several years earlier, so it was now standing empty. His house overlooked the beach at the delightfully named Beach Haven, and the property had its own swimming pool and jacuzzi, which we could use whenever we wanted.

Settling in, our first visitor was the former Worcestershire player Dipak Patel, who now resided in Auckland having married Vina, a native of New Zealand. Dipak also played for Birkenhead in between his international commitments for New Zealand, and it was a kind gesture to check if we needed anything. The Birkenhead club were looking forward to a great season. Having never won the championship, they sensed they had the nucleus of a squad that could do it this season, even though they would lose both Dipak and John Bracewell to first-class and international cricket from time to time.

Our opening fixture was a Saturday friendly in TePuke, about 60 miles south. Dipak picked us up in his Mercedes, which he'd had flown over from England. The countryside was beautiful, lush and green. New Zealand is about the same size as the UK but with a population of three million, a third of them in the Auckland area. I also learned there were around 26 sheep for every person there!

Rugby matches had left the ground quite badly damaged, so we played on an artificial surface, and it's probably fair to say the opponents were better hosts than cricketers. I took a wicket with my very first ball in New Zealand, and they were bowled out quickly. It was one of the shortest matches I've ever played, as we quickly knocked off the runs.

The following Monday, I received my sponsored car from Auckland Motors, a Mitsubishi Mirage Estate. Kate could drive it as well, so we took turns getting to know the area and spent a lot of time with Vina and her daughter, Alysha. It was still two weeks before the first competitive match, but training was twice a week, and I started my coaching commitments at some local schools. Most had rugby union as their first love, but the kids all seemed to enjoy the cricket sessions, and my groups ranged from sixth formers down to primary school students, with both boys and girls getting involved. Naturally, I was hoping I could repay my new club with some match-winning performances and couldn't have asked for a better start. Over the course of the weekend, I took 7-15 and then 5-20 as we won our opening fixture with ease, sitting pretty at the top of the table after the first round of matches. By now, my thoughts were already drifting towards the next English season and where I would be playing my cricket. Declaring my availability had been an astute suggestion from Mr Duff and had attracted lots of interest. Since arriving in New Zealand, I'd received offers from Glamorgan, Middlesex, Nottinghamshire, Somerset, Surrey, Sussex, and Warwickshire. Lots of counties were interested, but I couldn't make up my mind. Each had their attractions, and it weighed on my mind as I tried to decide what would be best for my career.

Warwickshire was Worcestershire's next-door neighbour, and many supporters regularly watched both teams. The advantage of going there was that I wouldn't have to move house, but I'd already decided leaving Worcestershire would release me from the rut I'd found myself in. I didn't consider Glamorgan for too long as the wickets had never suited me at Sophia Gardens. There were some attractions to joining Sussex, as I was sure I'd play lots of cricket for them, but I felt they were several players away from challenging for titles. Somerset said they were interested in including me in their rebuilding plans, but I was sceptical after how they'd rid themselves of those two great West Indians, Viv Richards and Joel Garner. The chance to play regularly at Lord's made Middlesex an interesting proposition in a side packed with experience; but the issue would be the number of fast bowlers already on the staff. Whilst I would always back myself, it might be tougher to command a first-team place week in and week out. I'd heard whispers around dressing room ill-discipline at Surrey, but you never really know about these things until you experience it yourself. I also liked the look of the coaching structure at The Oval, so I definitely wasn't ruling them out.

Things had gone well for Birkenhead; by Christmas, we were 10 points clear at the top of the table, and I was the leading wicket-taker. Competitive cricket was on a three-week break, so Kate and I decided to pack the car up and spend some time travelling around New Zealand. This would give me more time to decide which county to join for 1989.

Our first stop was at Taupo, where we booked into a cabin on the shores of the lake. From there, it was on to Napier, Wellington and then a ferry from North Island across to South Island on Christmas Day. I tried several times to phone mum in Barbados, but all the lines were engaged, so I just hoped my card and letter had arrived in time. We spent time in Nelson and Greymouth before arriving in the adventure capital of Queenstown, where we stood and watched the youngsters queuing to bungee jump off the bridge. Deciding that was far too dangerous, we took a cable car to the top of the mountain and had lunch and watched others water-skiing and parachuting before deciding we'd have a go on the jet boats. There was so much to do and see as we travelled down the South Island, stopping to explore caves before dolphin-watching at Milford Sounds. We visited a castle in Dunedin, then stopped off in Canterbury to see some friends from the club.

Nearing complete exhaustion, we arrived back at our flat after 19 days away, having done a total of 4,526 kilometres. I'd no sooner gotten back when the phone rang.

I had been avoiding phone calls from both Middlesex captain Mike Gatting and Surrey coach Geoff Arnold, and Kate was getting more and more agitated at my indecision.

Kate answered. As usual; she was under instructions to tell everyone I was not around. She arrived with the phone and said, 'A man on the phone says it is Dessie and he is a mate of yours?' Just then, I could hear that unmistakable laugh of my mate Desmond Haynes. 'Hi Ricky, it is Dessie; Gatt told me to give you a ring and let you know I have signed for Middlesex.' Now Desmond and I went back a long way; we grew up less than a mile from each other, we played for the same Barbados cricket club, Carlton, we drank in the same rum shop, played cricket on the beach together, I had known 'Joe Louis', as we called him in the village, all my life. This was the deal-breaker. I said to Dessie, 'Tell Gatt I'll sign'.

My mind was made up. I would sign for Middlesex, though I knew I'd have to work extremely hard to secure my place.

Before my contract arrived from Middlesex, I would have to have a medical and was referred to a doctor in West Auckland, who gave me a clean bill of health. Life was good, and things were falling into place for us. Kate took up the job offer, working as a computer operator for a paint manufacturing company.

Soon after arriving in New Zealand, I started learning to fly at Dairy Flats Aerodrome north of Auckland and was looking forward to getting my pilot's licence. Having led the table throughout, Birkenhead won the championship with victory over Waitamata. It meant we could enjoy the final match against the university with just our unbeaten record to protect.

Then, it happened. I was the leading wicket-taker, finishing with a five-wicket haul to reach 60 wickets for the season, but with the match almost won, I felt an uncomfortable, painful feeling.

From just one delivery, the sharp agonising pain had returned. I couldn't believe it; I'd just been given a clean bill of health!

My contract with Middlesex had been agreed, but would I be able to honour it? Kate shared my concerns and, as I hadn't seen Mum for over a year, we decided to fly to Barbados. It would also give Mum a chance to meet my sweetheart for the first time.

Before leaving Auckland, we were thrown a farewell party by the club. New Zealand had been very good to us. We'd seen most of the country during our travels, Kate had earned quite a bit of money from her job, and I was also the proud owner of a private pilot's licence. The cricket had gone well, though my overriding concern as I left the country was about the probable recurrence of my back injury.

On the way to Barbados, Kate was very nervous about meeting my family and Mum in particular. I was looking forward to seeing her after such a long time, and that excitement grew as we descended into Bridgetown. Looking out of the cabin windows, I was able to point out some of the big hotels as we flew along the west coast, but I sensed Kate was preoccupied with other thoughts. It felt great to be back home, it was just after midday, and the warmth of the sun hit me immediately as we walked across the tarmac. Approaching passport control, I could see some of my family waiting, but they would have to wait a little longer because one of our bags was missing. A baggage handler disappeared to check for us but returned with the bad news. There were no more bags to unload, and the plane had already started push back for a quick getaway to Trinidad, its next destination. Kate started to cry. The bag contained some of my kit and an assortment of presents she'd bought in New Zealand and Miami for our families. Eventually, we made it through customs, and there was Mum. I gave her a big hug and introduced her to Kate. She could immediately tell Kate had been crying. We told her about the bag and the missing presents so Mum told her not to worry.

I had booked a hire car to use during the week and spent the journey back to the village pointing out tourist spots and some of the better beaches to Kate, who was now looking forward to relaxing in the sun. As we entered the house, Kate whispered that everyone in the street seemed to be looking at me. I told her it was normal when visitors came around. The following day we headed off to see a few places I thought Kate would enjoy, and we stopped off in Bathsheba to see Norma and her kids before enjoying some delicious homemade lemonade. Then we travelled down the west coast before popping back to try one of Mum's specialities, a lovely Barbadian dish of yams, sweet potatoes, eddoes (a tropical vegetable) and dumplings with salt fish; all washed down with mauby, a refreshing soft drink made from the bark of the mabi tree. We then all piled into the car and travelled to Payne's Bay for a swim. It was just after 5pm, and the bright red sun was starting to drop slowly out of the sky, glittering on the water as it did so. The water was so clear and inviting and it took Kate totally by surprise at how warm it was.

'I want to live here forever,' screamed Kate, which was nice to hear, as I'd hoped she would fall in love with Barbados, like so many others before and since.

I had a little run along the beach, leaving the others to splash around in the shallows. It was nothing more than a gentle jog. But then …

…discomfort in my back kicked in.

The county season was only a couple of weeks away. Perhaps Mum had an old-time remedy that would help.

The following day, during a breakfast of mangoes with lemon juice and fried plantain, 'Bee Wee' phoned to say our bag had arrived from Miami and we could collect it. Kate was very pleased, as she had been made to wait to give everyone their presents, but her excitement soon disappeared: the clothes and gifts were missing, presumably stolen. Kate again burst into tears; she was so upset about losing her things. To cheer her up, I showed her some of the island's nightlife. We met my past under 19 roommate Hendy Wallace and his girlfriend, Joel, at The Ship Inn Pub in St Lawrence Gap, where a live band were performing. It was very noisy, but the atmosphere was excellent, and soon Kate had forgotten about the stolen stuff and was stamping her feet to the music of local band Second Avenue.

We eventually headed home at 5am. Mum was still awake, which made me feel a little guilty, but she said she just wanted to make sure we were OK and got home safely.

For our final day, I booked us all on the Jolly Roger, the legendary pirate ship that takes holidaymakers on a trip up and down the coastline. We left the marina around 10am and sailed past the harbour with calypso music blasting out. The ship sailed along the west coast and docked at Holetown, where the first settlers went ashore. There, we all had a barbeque while the crew made some of the passengers walk the plank, swing the rope or take part in a traditional pirate wedding. Our hosts served up some rum – deliciously sweet but also pretty lethal, and it wasn't too long before Kate began to feel the effects.

The following day, the family came to the airport to wave us off. There were lots of hugs and kisses for Kate, who had fitted in exceptionally well. Everyone had been anxious about whether she would take to life in the village, but she really enjoyed herself. Mum told me how much she liked Kate and was so pleased I'd found someone like her to share my life with. It had been a monumental six months; we had done so much together, and I knew Kate was looking forward to getting home to tell her friends and family about our adventures. If one thing had come out of it, we knew our relationship was solid, and I could finally put my relationship with Joyce to bed. There had been the odd disagreement but nothing major, and we were now not only lovers but the very best of friends. It was soon time to go. Time to face reality! And that was the discomfort I was feeling in my back. It felt eerily similar to my pain in 1985 but now on the left side.

CHAPTER 15

ON THE COMEBACK TRAIL

Clearing customs at Gatwick airport on a very dull morning, we were pleased to see Mr Clarke waiting.

All was not well, however.

'I have got very bad news for you, Ricky. Mr Duff is very ill in hospital, and we don't think he is going to make it.'

At the beginning of the New Year I'd written to him, telling him I'd decided to join Middlesex, and he'd replied, saying what a good decision he thought it was. That was our last correspondence.

As we drove towards Mr Clarke's house, thoughts about Mr Duff rushed through my mind. The day he'd first met me at the airport, his chuckle as he entered our study, how he'd wish us a happy birthday with tea and chocolate hobnobs, and getting me a pass in physics. He was a very kind and fair man, and I owed him so much.

The first thing I did on reaching Mr Clarke's house was to phone Sheila Duff and express my sadness at the news. She explained it was cancer and that he had gradually worsened over the last two years. He'd had several stays in the hospital but had wanted to keep it quiet. He had bravely fought the battle on his terms, but the latest hospital visit had indicated the end was near.

Our immediate plan was to put my house on the market and look at buying a flat in London. Kate would have to find a job. I was looking forward to meeting my new team-mates and playing for a new team but knew I'd have a fight on my hands to get into a very strong Middlesex first team. However, I was confident I could do it…

…provided I didn't have any back issues!

During a brief few days spent at Kate's mum in Staffordshire, I called the Middlesex cricket office and explained I was back in the country and would need somewhere to stay. They called back almost immediately to confirm we'd been booked into the Clive Hotel in Primrose Hill, 10 minutes from Lord's. After checking in, we discovered we'd been given a beautiful top-floor suite overlooking Regent's Park. My first day with the club was spent at the Barclays Sports Ground in Ealing.

Mike Gatting, the club captain, introduced me to the other team members, and we enjoyed a relatively light first training session. A few weeks of rest seemed to have done the trick as I was pain-free, and those first few days were extremely enjoyable.

However, on the Wednesday of the second week, when we moved to the Middlesex indoor school in Finchley, it happened again after the first session bowling indoors.

I could feel some discomfort.

Bowling a little slower because of the hard surface and managing a fairly light workload, I got through the session and was grateful to Kate for a massage before bedtime. I prayed I'd be fit for the season and have no recurrence of the injury. However, after each day's training, I knew it was hurting more and more.

Kate started a job temping for *The Daily Telegraph* and we moved out of the hotel and into Hillside Court, a rented flat on the Finchley Road. It was beautiful and had become available after the owners, a Greek couple, had taken six months off to sail the Greek islands. Without my back issues, life would have been just about perfect. Instead, day after day, I was waiting for the hammer to fall. In desperation, I visited in turn an acupuncturist, a homoeopath, a chiropractor, an osteopath and an Alexander technique therapist. None provided relief, offering diagnoses ranging from one of my feet being longer than the other to eating on the wrong side of my mouth.

For our first pre-season friendly at Cambridge University, I travelled to the match with Paul Downton, the Middlesex and England wicket-keeper. We had a quick stretch and warm-up on the Fenner's outfield before heading to the practice area and immediately I was in pain.

How could I tell my new coach I was unfit to play after being with the team for only a few weeks? Somehow, I managed the fielding practice session but knew this situation was untenable, as every step back to the pavilion produced a stabbing pain.

This was to be my Middlesex debut. I should have been so happy. Now, I couldn't even envisage going onto the field, let alone bowling.

No one else knows of my predicament, of course. None of them would have noticed me hobble to the toilet, where I sat and burst into tears. Who could I tell?

Would anyone believe me?

Middlesex were batting first, so I had some time to compose my thoughts. Then, I figured if I had a bath, maybe it would ease the pain. Perhaps there would be some magical cure from the warm Cambridge water.

Alas, no.

I was about to break down again as I returned to the dressing room to find I wasn't alone. Roland Butcher, a fellow Barbadian and the first black cricketer to represent England, was also there and instantly knew something was wrong. I explained everything to him, and he insisted I tell Paul Downton, who was skipper for that match. I played it down and said I'd be alright. After Roland's innings, he noticed I was still distressed so he told Paul. The twelfth man was instructed to return me to Lord's to see the physio.

The wheels had been put in motion, and by the time I arrived at Lord's, my x-rays from New Zealand were being examined closely by the physio. He was concerned I was getting pins and needles; it meant my back had gone into spasm, and it could be very serious. An appointment was made to see the club's orthopaedic surgeon the following day, and I was sent back to Hillside Court by taxi, where Kate found me feeling sorry for myself when she returned from work.

Frank Horan, the orthopaedic surgeon, had come up from Sussex to see me and said he'd spotted a problem when he first saw my x-rays; but the club had insisted on proceeding with the signing. He took some new x-rays, which bore out his worst fears.

Vertebra 4 was slipping above vertebra 5.

He said that an operation would eventually be needed to stabilise it, but for the time being, he thought we could probably get away with immobilising the back to get rid of the spasm and then start an intensive programme to strengthen the muscles to hold the vertebrae in place. Optimistically, he said if all went well, I might even play some cricket before the season ended.

The following day I was sent to St Mary's Hospital in Paddington, where Sister Taggart fixed me another plaster cast. I'd vowed I would never have another one, but it was made very clear that I wouldn't be able to play again without it.

Back in the flat, I couldn't get comfortable and wondered why life was so unfair. Then, I remembered Mr Duff. What right did I have to sit here feeling sorry for myself when he was going through something much worse? I grabbed the phone and called him, listening to how brave that lovely man had been. I promised to visit him in Malvern as soon as possible.

That evening, again cocooned in plaster, I felt helpless and could see I was bringing Kate down with my negativity. She popped out to get a couple of videos and returned with a takeaway from our local Indian restaurant.

We laid on the floor together to eat, but I had only tasted a few mouthfuls when I started to feel poorly. The cast seemed to be getting tighter and tighter as my stomach swelled, and I was having difficulty breathing. Lying on the floor, I began to panic and became hysterical. Kate didn't know what to do, so she rang her mum, a doctor, for advice. Down the phone line, I was told to lie still and take deep breaths until I'd calmed down.

Things slowly began to return to normal, and she asked Kate to keep an eye on me. If the cast did start to tighten again, then she must call an ambulance. Laying on that hard floor became a way of life over the next few weeks. It was more comfortable than getting into bed and at least kept me flat. From there, I kept an eye on the opening rounds of the County Championship, following the scores on Teletext or Ceefax. Middlesex won their first match easily, but it was of little comfort; my days were long and boring whilst Kate was at work. Any sleep I managed was fitful, and I had completely lost my appetite. Every day I imagined something else was wrong, becoming totally paranoid about my health. Soon our relationship became strained, and we argued over the slightest thing. I had very few friends I could call on as they were all in Worcester. The decision to start a brand-new life in London was turning into a nightmare.

Eventually, my hand was forced. Five weeks after having the cast applied, the doctor requested to see me again. I was full of negativity, expecting to hear the same news as on the previous occasion (six more weeks...), but the doctor said he was encouraged by what he saw. The spasm had gone, and the majority of my movement had returned. Mr Horan declared I needed to strengthen my back muscles to keep the vertebrae in place. I was to start a training programme immediately, beginning the following day at the Seymour Leisure Centre. So began a period of running in the pool, which then progressed to swimming. After a few days, I'd advanced to swimming twice daily and then moved on to various back-strengthening exercises. By the beginning of June, I was outside, running on grass much quicker than expected. As my recovery progressed, so did our relationship. Once again, we were like any other happy couple, socialising and developing a wider circle of friends.

The acid test was how my body would react to bowling again.

On 7 June, I had my first gentle bowl, and there was no reaction. Increasing my speed daily, the coaching staff adjudged me ready to play my first match for Middlesex on 18 June against the Royal Air Force at Uxbridge. Again, there was no reaction, so it was off to Southampton next for a second XI one-day fixture. I pushed my body hard, bowling with plenty of pace throughout my 11 overs. I'd worn a back brace for those first couple of matches as a precaution, but I discarded it for the three-day fixture against Hampshire at Bournemouth. Things were going well, and I put in two long, quick spells in their first innings and another in their second. I felt a little stiff afterwards, but that was a normal reaction to three days of pretty intense exertion. There was no pain, and that was the key.

The first team were away in Worcester that weekend, with a County Championship match starting on the Saturday, then continuing on the Monday and Tuesday after pausing for a Sunday League fixture in between.

My Saturday was divided between the gym and the swimming pool as I continued my rehabilitation, but when I arrived home in the evening, Kate said the coach had rung and would call back later. We stayed in, but there were no more calls, so I dismissed it as him wanting a general catch-up. However, at 7am the following day, he called. A couple of players were injured, and I was asked to drive to Worcester to act as cover for the Sunday League game.

I'd never packed my kit so fast and rushed off after kissing Kate goodbye. At least, it was a familiar route. I couldn't help but see the irony of me perhaps making my Middlesex debut at my old ground. Though I was getting ahead of myself, I was only going as cover. Making good progress, I was soon driving through the Worcestershire countryside, recalling those happy days of sausage rolls and crisps in the car with David Banks. The Middlesex team were staying at the

Gifford Hotel, across the road from Worcester cathedral. I parked and walked in, finding most of the players enjoying a leisurely breakfast. I followed them to the ground, with my own house only a mile away – I decided to pop in and see it afterwards.

At New Road I was greeted by the same gateman I'd seen for almost all my seven years there. Lots of people said hello as I unpacked my gear and walked towards the pavilion, where another familiar face, Jack, the dressing room attendant, was waiting. Having become used to turning left once inside the door, I remembered to keep straight ahead towards the visitors' dressing room. Dumping my kit down, I popped up to see the seconds, many of whom were getting ready for afternoon games in the local leagues. The crowd was beginning to build as I wandered over to the nets, and my presence raised a few comments from some of the Worcestershire players, many of whom claimed to have heard I was out for the season, which made me think of that famous Mark Twain quote, *Reports of my death have been greatly exaggerated*. I had been told at the hotel that Norman Cowans was struggling and would have a fitness test once we'd arrived at the ground. That appeared to have taken place because Mike Gatting came over and said I was playing.

Everything had happened so quickly. In April I'd been put into plaster for five weeks, I'd started running outside on 1 June, had my first bowl on 7 June, and now 18 days later, I was in the Middlesex first team, making my debut. Ideally, I would have preferred us to bat first, so I could have a little time to absorb everything, but the captain came back from the middle and said we were bowling. He came across and said I would be bowling first change, so I had a little more time to prepare.

We made a strong start, and Worcestershire were 40 for three by the time I was tossed the ball, with Phil Neale and Damian D'Oliveira at the crease. I knew them both very well and had bowled to them many times. Phil, the captain, liked to play the ball inside out through the off side, so I didn't want to give him any width outside off-stump. On the other hand, Damian, the coach's son, liked to play the ball through the leg side, so I was more than happy to give him a little width.

Gaining confidence and bowling faster as my spell continued, I struck in my seventh over, having Phil caught at midwicket by

132

Simon Hughes for my maiden Middlesex first-team wicket. I finished with the respectable figures of 1-26 from my eight overs and felt I had done pretty well. Worcestershire was bowled out for 143. After tea, I watched as we swept to a reasonably comfortable five-wicket victory to make it a perfect day. Gatting congratulated me afterwards and asked me to head back to London and rest up for the next match, but I thought I'd stop off and see my house.

It was up for sale, but the recession had hit the housing market, and sales were slow. I suspected I might have to rent it out for now and put it back on the market when sales picked up. Back home, I took Kate out for dinner and told her about the day and how well it had gone. I felt more of an association with the team now that I'd played for them. Over the next two days, I followed their progress intently as they got the better of Worcestershire again to win the County Championship match by nine wickets. I claimed two wickets in a one-day NatWest Trophy match away at Durham and was then selected for my Middlesex first-class debut on 1 July, against Lancashire at Lord's. Individually, I had a decent game, taking 5-94 in the match, but collectively the team had something of a shocker, bowled out for 96 and 43 and losing by over 200 runs. However, we bounced back in the next game, defeating Derbyshire by 70 runs at Lord's before defeating Yorkshire at Headingley. In their first innings, I took my first five-wicket haul for Middlesex and added another in their second innings to take 6-69 in the match. Back in April, when the plaster was going on, I could never have imagined I would return to action so soon and have so much success.

However, I was starting to feel a little sore with all my exertions. The day after finishing at Headingley, we were batting first against Kent at Uxbridge; I spent the entire day lying on the couch in the physio's room whilst our opening batters put on 361 runs. During the second day, we declared at 458 for one, with Haynes on 206 not out. I opened the bowling and quickly took the first three Kent wickets as they were shot out for only 164.

We asked them to follow on, but during the tea interval, I could feel my back stiffening up and the return of pins and needles in my toes.

The physio asked that I take no further part; I feared the nightmare was about to start all over again. I was prescribed bed rest for two weeks, unable to go out and becoming increasingly depressed. My days were spent in front of the television, switching from channel to channel. At the end of two weeks, I was instructed to return to the club for training. Everyone must have been happy with what they saw because I was selected in the squad to travel to the west country for back-to-back matches against Somerset at Weston-Super-Mare and Gloucestershire at Cheltenham College. I wasn't chosen in the final XI for the game at Weston and spent three days working with the physio, running along the beach front and swimming in the hotel pool.

Kate came down for the weekend, and we spent a happy couple of days together, enjoying time on the beach and dining in a quiet fish restaurant. I'd kept an eye on Gloucestershire's match against Lancashire at Cheltenham and saw that the visitors had won with a day to spare, and the fast bowlers had taken all the wickets. That made me think I might be in with a chance of playing, so it wasn't a total surprise when the captain walked towards me on the morning of the game and gave me the good news. From the dressing room window, I saw the captains go out for the toss and observed Bill Athey, the Gloucestershire skipper, turn towards his players and swing his arm around. It meant Middlesex was batting, and I had time to relax and look around this beautiful school ground, with the boundary fringed by colourful marquees. I'd played here as a schoolboy for Malvern against Cheltenham College, but with all the spectators in attendance the ground was almost unrecognisable.

Middlesex were bowled out for 222 by late afternoon, and my stomach was filled with butterflies as I stepped up to bowl. Running in for my first delivery, I could feel myself panicking midway through my approach. Gathering myself, I pushed through with the delivery and made the batter play. By the close of play on that first day, I'd taken a wicket and felt more confident in myself and my body. Thankfully, the next couple of days went our way as well, and we won the match quite easily, with me finishing with three wickets.

After a fiery spell in the second-round NatWest Trophy match against Nottinghamshire at Uxbridge and a couple of wickets in a convincing win over Northamptonshire at Lord's, I headed for Southampton in good heart for the semi-finals of the NatWest Trophy against Hampshire. I travelled down with Desmond Haynes, and we headed straight for bed once we'd got there. The short distance from the hotel to the ground was lined with people going to the game, and we knew it would be a great atmosphere. Hampshire won the toss and put us into bat. We made 267 for seven, with Dessie and John Carr each getting 80. They started their chase badly, and I managed to pick up a couple of wickets, but they scored freely enough only to require 18 from the last 18 balls. Thankfully, they lost wickets, and we edged home by three runs.

As we headed back to the dressing room, the champagne corks began to pop, and several supporters joined us, celebrating the fact we'd gotten through to the final. The news came through we'd be playing Warwickshire, who had beaten Worcestershire in the other semi-final. Despite my performances, I was never guaranteed a starting place, and I was left out of the next match against Sussex at Hastings. We were staying on the seafront in the Royal Victoria Hotel, and on the morning of the game, Mike Gatting explained he felt the wicket would be slow, so he wanted to play another spinner. However, I was back in for the next match against Nottinghamshire at Trent Bridge and had match figures of 8-86. Proving my fitness in that match had been important as we were approaching the one-day final. My form had been pretty good, and some journalists were suggesting I might be a good option for the forthcoming England tour of West Indies.

CHAPTER 16
FINAL WOES

Saturday, 2 September 1989, the day of the National Westminster Trophy Final at Lord's between Middlesex and Warwickshire and one day after Alan Duff's memorial service. This competition had begun with an early morning phone call from the Rev Mike Vockins, the Worcestershire Club Secretary on 28 June.

As soon as I heard him, my hands began to shake. I knew what he was going to say.

'Ricky, I have got bad news. Mr Duff has died.'

This is supposed to be the most important day of my cricketing life to date. The one person instrumental in me leaving Barbados and all that has occurred to me since then would not be here to see it.

I drove to Lord's in a daze. At 8.30am, the ground was already filling up as I lugged my cases up to the dressing room and pushed the door open to find it full of Warwickshire players. Someone pointed out Middlesex had lost the toss for dressing rooms and were in the visitors, so I had to drag my case through the corridors and the numerous doors to the dressing room on the other side of the Lord's pavilion.

Most of our team was already there, so I had to find a peg and put my bags down. I walked onto the balcony and looked around the ground as all the stands filled up. Mr Clarke, Kate, her mum and a couple of their friends were coming to watch. Downstairs in the Long Room, there was far more noise than usual, and lots of well-wishers wanted to stop us and pass on their messages of good luck. Everyone was excited; this was a cup final, one of the traditional showpiece occasions of the English cricket season.

I can't tell you how or why, but the grass felt different as I stepped onto it; perhaps this was just cup final nerves on my part. We all went over and had a net on the nursery ground, then did fielding drills on the main ground before heading back to the pavilion to leave the captains to do the toss and TV interviews.

Once inside, all the players moved to the balcony to watch the toss and then turned to the television to see the outcome. Mike Gatting bent over, picked the coin up and the BBC interviewer, Ray Illingworth, moved forward to speak to him. He had won the toss, Middlesex would bat first, and the team was the same as for the semi-final.

I watched our innings unfold on the TV in the dressing room and could tell from the off it would be a low-scoring affair. The wicket was slow and suited the Warwickshire attack, with only Desmond reaching 50 as we mustered 210 for seven from our 60 overs. Would it be enough? We were about to find out. Gatt gathered us around for some last-minute instructions, emphasising the importance of making a good start with the ball. Then we headed out.

Even navigating our way out to the pitch felt different to normal, as we were coming down the stairs on the away side of the pavilion. Through the Long Room we walked, boosted by plenty of applause, and then it was out onto the field. As a crescendo of sound went up, I looked around; the Home of Cricket was packed, as confirmed by the sign on the scoreboard:

TODAY'S ATTENDANCE: 30,000.

Most of them seemed to be cheering for us, but there was the odd group singing their hearts out for Warwickshire. They couldn't have served up a better atmosphere between them.

Gatt had already asked me to take the first over from the Pavilion End, and as I marked my run, I felt a sense of panic welling up inside again. However, I quickly dispelled any negative thoughts as a hush came over the ground, and the umpire called, 'Play.' I ran in and bowled a good length delivery which the batter let go by. A chorus of 'Well bowled, Ricky' emanated from the slip cordon, and I felt much better. The opening over was a tight maiden, I felt I was in the game, and as I moved to the boundary edge at the end of the over, that section of the crowd broke out into applause.

Warwickshire made a slow start and were well behind on the scoreboard as we broke for tea. Things were looking good, but the interval did us no favours as our opponents increased the tempo afterwards. The game see-sawed backwards and forwards; they would score freely for a while, and then we would halt the momentum with a wicket. Eventually, it all came down to the final over, with ten runs required. By now, it was starting to get dark, but the crowd were on the edge of their seats, and the noise was deafening. Simon Hughes was entrusted with bowling the final over, as he had done throughout the competition. At the crease were Asif Din, a senior player, alongside Neil Smith, a relatively inexperienced youngster in that Warwickshire middle order. Din took a single from the first ball, bringing Smith onto strike. Desmond had joked during an earlier break in play about the accessories he could buy for his new Mercedes with the win bonus. We were confident Smith was unlikely to hit Simon for six, but that's exactly what he did. Swinging hard and high, he made a solid connection, and I initially thought he had hit it straight to me, but as I positioned myself on the long-off boundary, it sailed over my head and into the crowd. The first six of the day, and it had come at such a crucial time. I looked in Desmond's direction, only for him to mouth the words, "Spoilers gone". With just three needed, the writing was on the wall. Some of the crowd began to inch closer to the boundary rope, intent on rushing onto the field at the end. The police and stewards were trying to control them and kept pushing them back, but the numbers were swelling and proving more and more difficult to contain. There was a long delay as Gatt tried to get as many players on the boundary as possible and in the correct position, but with a couple of balls to spare, they scampered the winning runs, and we were left feeling deflated as the Warwickshire players and supporters punched the air with joy.

It was very quiet in the dressing room, with no one quite believing how the trophy had been snatched from us. A few people were staring into space, one or two in tears. But, at times like those, it is all about the winners, rightfully enjoying their success, and the Warwickshire supporters were gathering on the outfield to watch the presentation ceremony. It was hard for some of our team to bear, and all I could do with my loser's medal was toss it into the bottom of my kit bag. I couldn't help thinking this day started with the worst possible thoughts and hadn't gotten any better.

There was almost a full week before the next match, so I drove up to Worcester to see Mrs Duff and sat and talked for a while, enjoying a cup of tea and a few hobnobs as we looked out over the college football fields. While in Worcester, I arranged for the house to be rented and spent a few days catching up with some old friends.

Our penultimate match of the season was against Sussex at Lord's starting on 8 September. We couldn't win the Championship so the season had gone a little flat, though we could still finish third and earn some prize money.

Sussex won the toss and batted first, making 313 for four on the first day, with me getting a couple of late wickets. The following morning, I arrived at the ground early before proceeding to the nets for my warm-up. On the way back, I entered the Long Room, and a gentleman stopped me and said, 'Congratulations.' In response, I said, 'Thank you,' presuming he was congratulating me on the wickets the previous evening.

At the top of the stairs were a few of our players, and they all turned and began congratulating me, saying, 'Well done' and things like that.

I was completely baffled.

'You've been selected for the England team to tour West Indies.'

I couldn't take it in and wondered if it was some elaborate hoax. I phoned Kate, told her, then Mr Clarke and also Mrs Duff. How I wished Alan were still around to enjoy it with me. I couldn't wait to telephone Mum, but then I got a message – she'd heard and had rung to congratulate me.

Our last match was away against Kent at Canterbury. I travelled down with the team but didn't play. Kate and I had made plans to take a short holiday after the season and decided the cheapest option would be to travel to France by car. Whilst at Canterbury, a travel agent phoned the dressing room to say he was taking a tour to Barbados and would like two players to go along as guests. I quickly volunteered, knowing it was a chance to see my mum free of charge. The tour would be leaving on 2 October, so I also had time to go to France.

We left for Dover on 18 September and made our way from Calais down the country towards Lyon, where Kate's sister Sue, a doctor, lived with her husband, Tom. They had a restaurant there, Mister Higgins, which was tucked high up in the Croix-Rousse.

The sisters don't see each other often and had plenty to talk about while I chatted to Tom, a former public-school boy from Shrewsbury, a school I'd played against on many occasions. After two days in Lyon, we drove to Monte Carlo, a place I'd heard so much about and had always wanted to visit. It was extraordinary; every other car seemed to be a Ferrari, and only the very best yachts were allowed to moor in the marina. I had seen the Monaco Grand Prix on television and I enjoyed driving around the circuit in our beat-up Ford Fiesta, imagining the commentator calling out my name as I went past the casino, around Loews hair-pin, through the tunnel, around the swimming pool complex, around La Rascasse and back onto the straight to reach the finishing line. I might never be able to afford to live in such luxury, but at least I'd always be able to tell my friends I'd driven the Monaco Formula One circuit.

The following day we began our lengthy return journey and picked out a route that took us through other parts of southern France we wanted to see. We worked our way along the Mediterranean coast, enjoying the breath-taking splendour of Nice, Cannes and St Tropez before reaching Toulon and then Marseilles. For the first time I felt at home here, as I'd not seen so many black people anywhere else in France. Driving north, we arrived back at Sue and Tom's and enjoyed a lovely meal in their restaurant. We left Lyon and headed for Paris, where we planned to spend a few days. We sought out the popular hotspots, climbing to the top of the Eiffel Tower, queuing to see the Mona Lisa in the Louvre and cruising along the Seine.

Shattered after cramming so much into a whirlwind visit, we laid in our hotel bed reflecting on everything that had happened within the space of just a few short months. I'd missed half of the season with back pain, then turned my fortunes around to such an extent that I'd been selected for an England tour. And now we'd zig-zagged our way around France and seen so much. In the morning, it would be back to our flat on the Finchley Road, although I'd be there for just one night before I'd be off again, this time to Barbados.

Having crossed the channel from Calais, I was pleasantly surprised when I got off the ferry at Dover. The customs officer checked my passport and said, 'I wish you the best of luck in the West Indies.' He was obviously a cricket supporter, but his words made me feel so proud. From there, things were a bit hectic, having to unpack and repack for the following day's flight while Kate readied herself for her first day back at work. She was able to drop me off at the airport, and then I met up with Kevin, who had organised the trip. The group had a few cricket matches arranged, and I was looking forward to joining in – an opportunity to play a few matches before returning for the full England tour four months later.

When we walked into the terminal building after touching down in Barbados, I knew where Mum would be standing and I looked up to the window to see her, along with the rest of the family. I'd already arranged with Kevin I'd be going home and would meet up with the tour party at the hotel the following day. Having collected my bags, what I wasn't prepared for as I walked through the double doors was a line of media and photographers all wanting interviews and photographs.

A new road had been built since the last time I'd been back, making the journey home even quicker than usual. As we turned into the village, I couldn't see a single soul, which I thought odd. It was like a ghost town. Where was everyone? As we climbed up and over the small hill, I had my answer. They were all there, shouting and cheering for me. Music was blaring out, and as I got out of the car, everyone started to pat me on the back and shout kind things. I was expecting just to come home and have a quiet time with Mum, but the whole village had turned out, and they'd obviously been planning this welcome-home party for some time.

Inside the house, I could see the table was full to bursting with all sorts of delicious food and that a bar had been set up in the backyard. Champagne corks began to pop, and the chatter grew louder and louder as everyone celebrated my return. I wondered who had paid for it all. Some senior villagers made speeches, but it was about everyone having a good time. The revelry continued until the early hours of the morning, and by the time I finally got to bed, the sun was rising.

I couldn't get over what it meant to everyone in the village for me to be selected to represent England.

Over the next couple of weeks, I learned that not everyone felt like that.

'Traitor!'

I put it behind me. Most drowned out these voices, with those of that view told to shut up by others who said they were just pleased a local boy had been considered good enough to be selected for the 'Motherland.' They were all very interested to impart advice, particularly on how I should go about bowling to local hero and neighbouring villager Desmond Haynes. I was just glad to see Mum looking so well and that I was be able to enjoy her splendid cooking again. She told me how much she was looking forward to being at the Test match and how proud she'd be. Virtually everyone from the village said they'd be there; I began to worry I wouldn't be able to get hold of enough tickets to keep everyone happy. They'd been so good to me; I didn't want to disappoint anyone.

We lost all our games, but everyone enjoyed themselves, we were made to feel very welcome, and it was deemed a huge success.

I couldn't wait for my next visit to Barbados as a member of the England touring party to play a Test series against the mighty West Indies.

A stack of mail awaited my return, much of it sent by well-wishers. However, standing out amongst them was an envelope with the letters TCCB.

I tore it open.

The Test and County Cricket Board were the game's administrators, and they had sent me a programme to be followed until our tour departure. Standing out for me were two dates in particular. Training would start at Lord's on 1 November, and there would be a medical at the Edgbaston Health Clinic on 18 December. So, training was around a month away and the tour three months away.

Over the next few weeks, I worked through my fitness programme, spending a lot of time working out at the exclusive Cloisters Country Club in Stanmore. On our first day at Lord's, all the players from the southern region were there. Other clinics had been set up around different parts of the country. Our group of bowlers worked together alongside some former Test bowlers, whilst the batters did the same, working with their counterparts.

From the start, our training focused intensely on any weaknesses within the West Indies squad. Our batters spent their days playing off the back foot, and the bowlers bowled along the corridor of uncertainty. The TCCB brought in a trainer to get everyone as fit as possible, and we were taken to the Human Performance Centre at Lilleshall in Shropshire for a fitness assessment. Everyone was sent their personal fitness programme to adhere to before leaving for the tour. Between the squad sessions at Lord's and Molesey cricket ground in Surrey, I continued going to Cloisters Wood. As Christmas approached, I worked harder than ever, but there was still one big hurdle to overcome: the medical at Edgbaston. I drove up early in the morning and called in to see Mr Clarke in his office. He seemed delighted to see me, and we had lunch at Aston Villa Football Club. He told me how proud he was of my achievements and recalled the day, back in 1980, when the Malvern headmaster encouraged by Mr Duff approached him with the idea of sponsoring me. He said he'd felt it was the right thing to do and how delighted he was to have been part of my journey into professional sport. We laughed about some of the moments we'd had together and talked about the times when other public schools weren't happy about playing Malvern because of me. and when Worcestershire didn't think I was injured.

From there, it was on to my medical, and thankfully I was passed fully fit, meaning my drive back down the motorway was a pleasant one.

Six weeks from now, I would be going on tour with England.

CHAPTER 17
DREAMS SHATTERED

Tuesday, 23 January 1990. D day. Kate had agreed to drive me, and we'd decided to set off at around 6.30pm and have a leisurely drive around the M25 to reach the hotel in good time.

We were just about to leave when the phone rang. It was my Middlesex team-mate, Angus Fraser.

'What time are you leaving?' I instinctively asked.

'I'm already here, and we're wondering where you are. You were meant to be here by six, and everyone is waiting for you. The papers want to speak to you, and you've missed the team meeting.'

Now I was panicking; my first tour, and already I'd made a bad impression. Grabbing my bags, we drove there as quickly as possible, but it was still around an hour before I reached the hotel. Everyone started to laugh as I walked in. I'd had all day to get here and still turned up late! Over in the corner, I could see team manager Micky Stewart and captain Graham Gooch in discussion. I thought it best to go over and apologise straight away. They saw me coming.

'What happened, Ricky?' said Micky.

'I thought it said 8pm,' I replied.

'It did. But didn't you get the second letter telling you it had changed?'

I told him I hadn't.

'Don't worry,' said Micky. 'I'll tell you later what I said at the meeting, but I did tell everybody I'll give them two lives, and you've lost one of yours already!'

He was laughing as he said it, so I didn't know if I was in trouble or not!

The rest of the evening was spent signing a pile of sponsors' bats and autograph sheets, answering journalists' questions and posing for dozens of photographs. Eventually, it was time for dinner and a few quiet drinks with the other players and their wives before Kate and I retired to our room.

The early alarm had me in the shower before 6am, and then it was time to put on the tour blazer and tie. I recalled seeing the

England players back in 1981 and thinking how smart they looked. Back then, as a young Barbadian boy, I was hoping England would be beaten, but now I was returning to the Caribbean wanting to play my part in turning the tables on this formidable West Indies side. After breakfast, there was another photocall and yet more autographs to sign, and then it was time to walk Kate to the car and kiss her goodbye, knowing how much I'd miss her over the next couple of months.

Along with my new England team-mates, I enjoyed a short coach journey to the airport, full of laughter and excitement. We were whisked through passport control and had barely reached the duty free section before a booming announcement, 'This is the first call for flight BA255 to Antigua and Barbados; this flight is now boarding at gate 26.' Determined not to get into further trouble and lose my other life, I stuck close to the manager and followed him onto our Boeing 747 for the start of our journey.

This was it! I was now part of the following England squad heading out to the Caribbean to play the West Indies in a five-Test series:

GA Gooch (Essex), captain, AJ Lamb (Northants), vice-captain, RJ Bailey (Northants), DL Capel (Northants), PAJ DeFreitas (Lancashire), RM Ellcock (Middlesex), ARC Fraser (Middlesex), EE Hemmings (Nottinghamshire), N Hussain (Essex), W Larkins (Northamptonshire), DE Malcolm (Derbyshire), KT Medlycott (Surrey), RC Russell (Gloucestershire), G Small (Warwickshire), RA Smith (Hampshire). Tour manager – PM Lush and team manager – MJ Stewart.

After a 90-minute stop-over in Antigua, where we could disembark and walk around, we made the short hop to Barbados. There were so many emotions running through my head as I looked out of the window; it seemed no time at all since I'd made my first flight back to Barbados from school carrying a letter from Mr Duff to Mum and Dad.

The captain spoke over the intercom, 'Thank you for flying British Airways. I hope you had a pleasant flight, and we look forward to seeing you aboard British Airways again. Before I go, I would like to wish the England cricket team the best of luck on their tour. Thank you.'

There was lots of chatter and photographs and one or two welcoming speeches. Then, I heard someone say, 'Ricky.' I knew that voice so well. It was Mum, and I turned to give her a big hug as cameras flashed all around us. It made me so emotional to be with her, and I couldn't help but wish Dad had been there; Alan Duff, too, for he had made much of this possible.

From the start of the tour, I was again experiencing back pain. I nursed it along as much as I could, but it was clear I needed to prove my fitness in a strenuous net session at the Castries Cricket Ground in St Lucia on 7 February and the four-day warm-up match against the Windward Islands if I was to have a chance of playing in the first Test on 24 February.

As the net session progressed, I pushed myself harder and harder but could feel more and more discomfort in my back and legs. In the lead-up to the tour matches, the former England batter Geoff Boycott had written an article attributing my back pain to psychological problems. I was determined to prove to myself this was not in my mind and pushed on. However, towards the end of my bowling stint, I lost all feeling in my legs, and my back went into total spasm. Even before the team's medical staff had made their assessment, I knew my tour was over. My dream of playing Test cricket looked to be up in smoke. Now I had even greater concerns: Would I ever play again?

My preference would have been to return to Barbados and spend time with Mum, hoping the warm Caribbean sunshine would aid my recovery, but that decision was taken out of my hands, with the doctors insisting I return to England for treatment. It had been quite big news when we boarded our flight to begin the tour; now, I was slipping back into the country alone and, to a certain extent, ignored. Mind you; other things were going on in the world as 11 February saw Nelson Mandela released from prison after 27 years and Mike Tyson battered to defeat by Buster Douglas.

Confused, frightened and nervous about what lay ahead, I arrived back in England on 14 February and was whisked off to the Park Street office of orthopaedic surgeon Frank Horan. Over the next few weeks, Mr Horan and another world-renowned expert in the field of stress fractures, orthopaedic surgeon Johnny Johnson, conducted a series of tests and scans before diagnosing multiple stress fractures. I would need corrective surgery. The surgeons explained that with the fractures affecting L3, L4 and L5, spinal fusion was not an option as this would prevent me having the required mobility to continue as a fast bowler. My only option, I was informed, would be bone grafts – bone would be taken from the left hip and used to repair the fractures; the grafts would then be held in place by several titanium screws. Surgery was booked to take place at the Nuffield Hospital in Hove. I was extremely anxious, never having been under anaesthetic before. Kate's mum, Dr Marie Toft, was allowed to accompany me throughout the procedure.

Blinking back into consciousness, I came around after several hours of surgery and felt like a vice was holding me in position. I remember staring towards the ceiling and being aware of all the drips and drains attached to me. A wiggle of my toes brought a sigh of relief that I still had feeling. It had been a major concern the operation wouldn't go as planned and that I would end up paralysed. The surgeons stopped by my bedside and said everything had gone well, but they insisted I remain in the prone position for a couple of weeks to allow the healing process to begin. Foolishly, I had hoped to be pain-free, but it was the opposite, and as the first night wore on, I was in agony, only getting relief through pethidine. The ward matron advised I was only to call for this medication when I was at the limit of my pain threshold, as I was only allowed a limited quantity. After two weeks of lying on my back, things started to improve, and with the aid of a Zimmer frame and some understanding nurses, I could stand, despite dizziness, disorientation, and nausea.

Within a few more days, the drains and drips were removed, and I could take my first steps unaided. Satisfied with my progress, Mr Horan told me I could continue my convalescence at home, and once again I was fitted with a body cast. Free of the drips, drains, and unappetising hospital food, I faced another period of minimal movement and oppressive restrictions caused by the cast. Sitting down for long periods was impossible, as the smallest amount of food seemed to cause my body to swell to the point where breathing was restricted. Showering was also a major logistical exercise, with intermittent sleep and short walks extremely tiring. Worst of all, there was a permanent itch in the middle of my back that could only be reached with the help of a knitting needle.

Finally, the day arrived for me to get rid of my turtle shell, and the doctors were happy to hand my care back to the Middlesex CCC physio to prepare me for the new season. It would be a lengthy recuperation, but I was determined to prove my fitness and return bowling faster than ever.

A period of my rehabilitation was to be spent at the Defence Medical Rehabilitation Centre at RAF Headley Court, a facility known for its expert treatment of back injuries, expertise acquired from treating aircrew's ejection seat injuries. The extreme acceleration of an ejection seat would cause the same type of back injuries that could be identified in fast bowlers. My rehab began in the swimming pool, with me wearing a life jacket and treading water for most of the day. I soon progressed to running lengths in the pool and then into the weights room. The physios then eased me onto daily sessions on the treadmill, as well as doing hundreds of sit-ups and back hyper-extensions. Throughout the entire process, I had no back pain, although most of my other muscles became tender with the repetitive exercises.

At this time there was a major conflict in the Gulf region. Iraq had invaded and occupied Kuwait, which resulted in the coalition forces becoming involved. The reason I mention this is because Headley Court was a military medical centre, it was expected to house casualties; those of us that were classified as 'civilian inmates' were warned we might have to leave if numbers escalated. I would sit and talk to inmates as we watched the news coverage of the war. We watched in horror as Iraqi television paraded two British servicemen they'd shot down and captured, pilot John Peters and his navigator, John Nichol, who was known to many there.

Being so close to those involved gave me a different perspective on life. Then, a more personal loss hit home. RAF Wing Commander, Nigel Elsdon of 27 Squadron, a fellow Old Malvernian, was killed whilst flying a Tornado jet on a bombing raid over Iraq.

CHAPTER 18

ONE LAST ATTEMPT

The closer we drew to the 1991 season, the more convinced I was I wouldn't be ready in time. Players were returning from their overseas contracts, and all I had done was send down a few very gentle deliveries in the Middlesex indoor school at Finchley. Thankfully, I was still pain-free, but I was all too aware the most challenging time was ahead. Soon, they would want me to be bowling outdoors in the cold weather.

Things went slightly better than expected, but I could feel some discomfort. My workload had to be managed carefully, and coming back for second and third spells was proving difficult, but with the help of painkillers and anti-inflammatories, I pushed through it. Scans showed no apparent damage, and it was felt that the discomfort was probably the result of scar tissue, so I was urged to try and play through it. Exceeding all expectations, especially my own – I was included in the side to face Essex at Chelmsford on 2 May 1991. This was a one-day Benson and Hedges group match, and the club felt it was the perfect opportunity to ease me back in.

Mike Gatting was charged with managing my workload. The Essex team included Graham Gooch, captain of my ill-fated West Indies tour, and Nasser Hussain, who had been my roommate on the Barbados leg of that tour. Nasser had been shocked at me buying a bottle of WD40 and applying it to my back after a member of the Bajan public had phoned the hotel recommending it as a remedy for my back pain. It was nice to catch up with those two and even more satisfying to have Gooch caught behind by Paul Downton as my first List A wicket since my return. Things went pretty well, and I felt I was somewhere close to my top pace and it was a huge relief to come through the match unscathed.

My next game was in the 40-overs-a-side Refuge Assurance League, against Sussex at Hove, where I'd undergone my operation. Then it was on to Fenner's, where I'd already experienced one back spasm in 1989. I made it through both games without much discomfort, then sat out the next match against the West Indies tourists, although I was pleased to have a good catch-up with my old mate Desmond Haynes.

One of the best batters in the world, Dessie is a good friend and my team-mate for Middlesex and Carlton. We are also now next-door neighbours in both England and Barbados.

I played in the next couple of three-day matches, away trips against Sussex and Somerset but I could feel the pain returning. The four-hour drive from Hove to Taunton took its toll, and I was in agony by the time we arrived. Somehow, I managed to control the pain and bowl quickly, thanks to an ever-increasing assortment of pills. Amongst my haul of six wickets was that of the prolific South African Jimmy Cook. Anyone looking at my performances from the outside may have been impressed by the pace I was generating and my number of victims.

However, only I knew the truth: the pain was increasing with each performance.

Life was becoming untenable, and I was only getting through it by the sheer volume of painkillers I took. I must have been disguising things well and I was doing fine on the park because on 6 June I received a phone call, in the strictest of confidence, from England manager, Micky Stewart, advising me that he was considering me for the third Test, to be played against the West Indies at Trent Bridge a month later. I believe he was frustrated with my replacement on the West Indies tour, Chris Lewis, who had opted out of the first Test at the eleventh hour. In the weeks before that Test, he wanted me to play as many back-to-back games as possible to prove my fitness. My heart sank. With the pain I was in, I knew this would be a hurdle too far. I thanked Micky for bearing me in mind and promised to do my best to justify selection. Perhaps the weather gods would be kind, and there would be a few wash-outs during the remainder of June. Get through it, and my dream of playing international cricket would be a reality.

Armed with a new focus, I looked towards the next match, against Leicestershire at Uxbridge, one of Middlesex's outgrounds. I had a pretty good record there and a particularly happy memory of bowling a fiery spell at the Nottinghamshire and England opening batter Chris Broad. Nevertheless, it would be preferable for me if there was plenty of rain around, as it would strengthen my chances of getting through the next few weeks unscathed. On the morning of 7 June, I peeled back the blinds to discover one of the sunniest days of the year. However, I still retained hope I wouldn't have to push myself too hard, as the last time we'd played at Uxbridge, we had won the toss and batted for almost two days against Kent, amassing a score of 458 for one, with Desmond scoring 206 not out and Ian Hutchinson hitting 177. I had no doubt Gatt would want to do the same today.

Having taken my usual assortment of pills, I watched intently from the balcony as Gatt and the Leicestershire captain Nigel Briers walked out for the toss and smiled contentedly as Gatt appeared to win it. Great, I thought. Hopefully, I will have an extra day and a half of recovery time. However, that went out of the window as our skipper returned and announced he'd put them in. My stomach began to churn with anxiety, but I settled quickly into my work and by lunch had the respectable figures of 7-3-22-1, having dismissed Tim Boon.

Reflecting on the events of the opening session, I sat in our dressing room, only for my back to go into an immediate spasm. A feeling of nausea instantly swept over me, causing me to have hot and cold flushes, tunnel vision, and producing pins and needles in my toes. I was in absolute agony and could neither sit nor walk. My match was over. Transport was arranged to take me home, and I was picked up the following morning and taken to see Frank Horan in his Park Street office. Unfortunately, further scans were inconclusive, leaving him to speculate that perhaps a screw was protruding into a nerve canal. He decided a further operation would be necessary to enable him to file away the protruding screws. This wouldn't be as big an operation as before, but it would mean an end to my season and put paid to any chance I had of making the squad for the winter's World Cup in Australia and New Zealand.

Again, the operation would be carried out by Mr Horan, accompanied by Mr Jonny Johnson at the private Princess Grace Hospital in Marylebone. Mr Johnson had been a member of the Royal College of Physicians since 1971 and specialised in spinal spondylolisthesis, lower back pain, sciatica, and neck pain. He lectured at Imperial College School of Medicine and asked if he could use the scans of my original fractures as lecturing material. He felt they showed the earliest development of spinal fractures he had seen. Of course, I was only too willing to give him that permission.

My operation began at 9am, so I was understandably confused and disorientated when I woke at 10pm. The feeling of being clamped to the bed was back, and I was in severe pain. Where had all the time gone? I was expecting to leave the theatre within a couple of hours. The nurses were unwilling or unable to give me any information and advised me to await the surgeon's visit in the morning. I suspected I was being fobbed off.

Mr Johnson was due on the ward at 10am, and I lay awake most of the night wishing away the hours until I could speak to him. Sleep was impossible, partly because of my back discomfort but also because I feared what I might be told. The surgeon arrived on time and was giving nothing away by his demeanour. With a poker face, he asked three questions at once.

'How are you? Did you sleep well? How is the pain?'

He then began checking the drain and the drips as I asked him why it had taken so long.

'We found a lot more damage than anticipated,' he said. 'The bone grafts had not taken, and gristle had formed instead of new bone growth. It's not as strong as bone, so a number of the screws had broken, causing severe damage. Those screws had to be drilled out and both bone grafts and screws replaced.'

I asked why this kept happening to me.

'Rick, as human beings, we were never supposed to walk upright,' he began. 'Not only are you walking upright, but you are sprinting, jumping, twisting, slamming one foot down followed by the other and then decelerating rapidly. That produces enormous stress, which ends in your lower back.'

I just about got the next words out,

'Will I be able to continue playing?'

'Of course,' he said. 'But this could recur. And I wouldn't recommend any further operations.'

Over the next few weeks, I had plenty of time to contemplate my future, with little else to occupy my mind as I stared up at the ceiling. At 26 years of age, I had undergone two major operations and battled through three strenuous rehabilitation programmes, with another imminent. I had been encased in three plaster cast cocoons and would have to wear another one when I left the hospital. Furthermore, I had had several cortisone injections and a daily regime of painkillers and anti-inflammatories.

On the one hand, I had shown I could battle back from adversity, and I was still young enough to fulfil all of my cricketing ambitions, but on the other, I was asking myself, 'Am I physically, mentally, and emotionally strong enough to go through it all again?'

Whilst I was having these thoughts, over and over again, I was visited by Colin Tomlins, who was the physical trainer for the 1990 West Indies tour. He kindly brought me a vast amount of fruit and chocolate and *The Book of Heroic Failures*, telling me it was ideal for someone who needed a bit of a lift. A further boost came when I received a phone call from Micky Stewart, giving me encouraging words and a promise he'd call in to see me soon. That made my mind up. I'd come too far to give up without another fight. Sure, I wasn't looking forward to learning to walk again, the weeks of plaster cast, treading water, weights, miles of running and learning to bowl fast once more, perhaps with a change of action this time. But I could almost taste international cricket. I'd been so close to making my debut in the West Indies and then again at Nottingham. Perhaps it would be third time lucky.

My latest bout of rehab would be undertaken at a fitness club in Stanmore owned by the former Middlesex and England left-arm spinner Phil Edmonds. My team-mate, Gus Fraser was also side-lined, hoping to make his recovery from a hip injury, so we teamed up for our daily sessions. Gus has always been blessed with great mental strength, so he was terrific to have as a training partner. His presence made the sessions less tedious and more competitive. As a bowling colleague, he was never the quickest, but you knew he would always give 110 per cent. In 1989 when I was bowling at my quickest, Gatt was always shouting, 'Ricky give me five of your fastest overs, don't worry about runs, and then you can fuck off and have a shower. If we need to pull it back, I'll get Gus or Ernie (John Emburey) on to do that.'

As a fast bowler, I found that freedom very liberating. It was a direct contrast to my years at Worcester and the lack of clear instructions from the captain there. Training sessions with Gus were always highly competitive, full of banter and fun. He supports Liverpool

FC, and I have supported Spurs since the 1981 FA Cup final, when Ricky Villa left a mark on my young life, probably forever. Villa, an Argentine international, scored one of the greatest goals Wembley has ever seen to help his side win the trophy. Apart from our mutual love of football, Gus and I were big fans of the rock band Queen and we were genuinely saddened to return from a training run to hear of the death of lead singer Freddie Mercury. Queen and The Jam had always been a staple of the music played in School House at Malvern College.

Thanks to Gus and the band of physios and trainers who helped me along the way, my rehab went well, and as the 1992 season approached, I was beginning to feel as fit as I had ever done, or at least as fit as I had for many years. Middlesex had arranged pre-season training at the Quinta do Lago Club on the Algarve on the south coast of Portugal. On the British Airways flight down to Faro, the captain kindly allowed me to sit on the flight deck for the landing. I absolutely loved it, and it brought back all my early ambitions of one day becoming an airline pilot.

During the stay, I was considered fit and raring to go, but as soon as I turned my arm over, I could feel discomfort. As before, it was nothing too serious at first and was completely manageable with the help of painkillers and anti-inflammatories. There weren't any spasmodic episodes, but at the end of each session, I could feel sciatic pain running down my right leg. The consensus from the club's medical staff was it might be scar tissue. I knew differently. Having had several episodes of back pain stretching back into my teenage years, I'd become attuned to the circumstances that led up to each major event. They usually began with sciatica and heavy legs, then progressed to lower stomach pain, groin pain, pins and needles. Then I would have sweats, hot and cold sensations, tunnel vision and finally, nausea and vomiting. As I finished another session and began vomiting, I knew where this was heading…

I had reached the end of the road.

The next morning at breakfast, I told Gatt of my decision to retire. His immediate reaction was to ask if I was sure. I was. He'd seen how much agony and torment I'd gone through and knew I meant it. All I wanted to do was get back to London and lock myself away; I didn't want to see or talk to anyone else. Gatt promised the club would make an announcement to the press. Kate picked me up at the Grace Gates and drove me back to the flat, where I got undressed and went straight to bed.

As the days passed, I found it harder and harder to leave the bed. The blinds were almost permanently drawn, and our relationship became increasingly strained. It became a source of daily embarrassment to have Kate return from work to find I hadn't even managed to get dressed. I became concerned about my health – I always had headaches and they appeared to be getting worse. The more I focused on those, the more debilitated I felt. Was my eyesight failing as well? I seemed to have lost my peripheral vision and now had tunnel vision. I scoured the medical books to diagnose the cause of these symptoms. Over a short period, I became convinced I also had other issues. My heart was beating faster than normal; at certain times of the day, it went into overdrive, almost beating out of my chest. I was totally exhausted, with no energy. I tried to cut things out of my diet, but that had no effect, and I couldn't sleep at night but was sleeping all day. Kate felt I wasn't getting enough fresh air as I rarely went outside, but I couldn't see how that would affect my racing heart, or help my daily headaches and failing vision. It seemed pretty obvious to me that a brain tumour was at the root of all my troubles. I went along with the notion that perhaps I could help myself more, but a step or two outside quickly brought things to a head. Walking to the junction of Narcissus Road and Mill Lane, I was plunged into doubt and confusion. Not sure where I was or where I was going, I had a sudden urge to jump in front of the oncoming traffic.

Thankfully, something prevented me, and I snapped back into reality. I made it back home and broke down in front of Kate. With two doctors in her family and several of her mum's friends being doctors, she sought immediate help.

She drove me to her mother, who listened as I poured out the list of things I thought were wrong with me. Then I told her I'd done a bit of self-diagnosis and was convinced it was anything from HIV to a brain tumour, food allergy to cancer. Whatever it was, I was sure it was terminal. Dr Toft took me to her surgery, conducted various tests, and told me to go home and try to relax whilst she got to the bottom of it.

A few days passed, leading me to believe it could only be the worst news. Then she wanted to see me.

'Ricky,' she said. 'All of your tests are normal. I think you are suffering from depression. You have been forced to stop doing something you have done all your life.

'All of this is in your mind,' she continued.

I wasn't so sure.

'What about my racing heart.'

'Panic attacks.'

'What about my vision and headaches?' I asked.

'Look,' said Marie, 'Just months ago, you were running miles, swimming, lifting weights and bowling. Do you think anyone could do that and be terminally ill?'

She suggested I take some time away, forget about cricket, and try to relax. I had hoped she would be able to find a root cause of my problems, but she was quite emphatic that – my back issue apart – I was basically in good health and was very unlikely to keel over any time soon.

Was it time to prove my dad's theory wrong? Could black men fly aeroplanes?

CHAPTER 19

FLYING HIGH

As a 12-year-old, I had sat on the Harbour Road Wall and watched the American Navy landing fighters on an aircraft carrier. When I heard about visits for school kids, I was first in the queue. A barge arrived, and soon I was in the bowels of this enormous ship, heading to the flying area. I had found my calling. Just then, the tour guide asked if anyone wanted to sit in the aircraft. 'Of course.' I sat in the cockpit and instantly knew I wanted to fly aeroplanes, but I had no money, and cricket was becoming the focus.

Then, in May 1988, I was frustrated with Worcestershire's selection policy and decided I needed to learn to fly. My nearest flying club was Shobdon, an airfield near Hereford and pretty soon I was up in a Cessna 152, spending more than an hour flying around the local area before landing with a smile. I knew this was something I wanted to pursue.

I spent the 1988 off-season at Beach Haven, Birkenhead, on Auckland's north shore. My landlord Frank, an old New Zealand Air Force pilot, learned of my love of flying and recommended I visit the Dairy Flats aerodrome, 20 miles north of Auckland.

On 14 October 1988, I started my private licence, the aircraft also a Cessna 152. By 2 December 1988, I had done 10 hours total time. Instructor Brett Moffit stepped out of the aircraft and said, 'Do one circuit for me'. Ever since sitting in the cockpit of the American fighter, I had craved this. As I positioned the aircraft downwind, I had a few moments to take it in. I looked to my right; the seat was empty. I was doing this all alone. Minutes later, I was on the ground safely, my first solo flight completed.

With Dr Toft's advice in my head, I set out to prove Dad wrong.

In September 1992, my injury compensation pay-out from the insurance company was sitting in an escrow account. I had applied to the Aero Mech flying school in Scottsdale, Arizona and allocated £25,000 to fund my American flight training. The exchange rate leading up to September was $2 to the pound.

On the morning of Tuesday, 15 September, George Soros's Quantum Fund began a massive sell-off of sterling. The rules of

157

the Exchange Rate Mechanism required the Bank of England to accept any offers to sell sterling. The morning after, Chancellor of the Exchequer Norman Lamont and Robin Leigh-Pemberton, the Governor of the Bank of England, began buying sterling to prop up the currency. With Soros's Quantum Fund selling sterling faster than the Bank of England could buy it, John Major's Government decided the next option was to increase interest rates in the hope speculators would be tempted to buy sterling. Rates rose from 10% to 12% to 15%. Despite this, dealers continued selling sterling, and by 7pm that evening, Britain had crashed out of the ERM. Black Wednesday 1992, and the pound was in freefall against the dollar.

My former Middlesex colleague Angus Fraser now works for Patrick Whittingdale Fund Management, a sponsor of the England cricket team. Learning of my plight, Mr Whittingdale, who had supported plenty of England youngsters such as Nasser Hussain and Martin Bicknell, bought the £25,000 in dollars and waived his fees in lieu of me receiving my pay-out. By then, the pound had fallen to $1.68. Instead of the $50,000, I would now have $42,000. When my training began in January 1993, the pound was at $1.50.

My American training began on 19 January, a familiarisation flight in a Cessna 152. Ground school and flying syllabus completed, I took my American PPL on 2 March at the Stellar Airpark Chandler, Arizona.

With my newly acquired American PPL, I flew to Lake Havasu, the spring break location of Western American colleges and universities. It is best known for being the location of the old London Bridge. The bridge was purchased by the American entrepreneur Robert Paxton McCulloch for $2.46m, taken apart brick by brick, shipped to California and trucked to Lake Havasu, where it was reassembled. It was said McCulloch thought he had bought the more impressive Tower Bridge.

Next up, instrument training. The aircraft of choice was the Cessna 172. My training partner was the Belgium Bart Beelen, who promised to teach me Flemish, and I vowed in turn to teach him Bajan. This segment formed the basis of any commercial pilot, the ability to control an aircraft purely by reference to instruments. All flights were flown in clouds, and if clear skies prevailed, a blind was used to prevent sight out of the cockpit.

Building hours as part of the course was an opportunity to see some of America. The C-172 has a range of around 750 miles, bringing into play the Pacific Ocean in the west, to Salt Lake City in the north, Odessa, Texas, in the east and Chihuahua, Mexico, in the south.

The most important part of instrument flying is the predetermined manoeuvres to transfer from instrument flight to a point where a visual landing can be made. It is a challenge to master these procedures as well as navigating and communicating.

My FAA instrument rating check ride was carried out on 21 May at the Deer Valley Airport. Next was the commercial licence, which allows a pilot to be paid for their work.

My commercial pilot rating began on 3 June. The syllabus included learning professional cross-country day and night procedures, building cross-country experience, flying complex aeroplanes and flying commercial manoeuvres such as steep turns, steep spirals, lazy eights, chandelles, eights on pylons and all the different types of take-offs and landings.

I sat my American commercial check ride on 13 July.

Next up was the multi-engine instrument course in the Beechcraft Duchess. It seems odd to fly a twin-engine aircraft but to spend most of the course on one engine, practising asymmetric flight. Having mastered this, you must master it under instrument rules. On 4 August, I passed my MEI rating at the Goodyear Airport.

I had entered the United States on a J-1 student visa, which allowed me to remain for two years as a student, flight instructor or charter pilot. However, to use the privilege of my J-1, I had to acquire my instructor qualification.

On 8 August, I started my Certified Instructor rating. This course was mainly classroom-based, with the highlight being the check on spin recognition and spin recovery. This can be distressing for some students. The aircraft is repeatedly climbed and spun in both directions. The student must recognise the conditions that will lead to a spin, the direction of the spin, the number of turns and the correct actions to enable recovery from the spin. For this lesson, you are encouraged to carry a few sick bags!

By the end of the course, I had a healthy respect for the type and number of errors student pilots can make. And in this environment, small mistakes can quickly escalate into fatal ones. As my flight school training ended, I promised to be as diligent as possible in my flying career. I could now be paid to pilot an aircraft. To have the same privileges in the UK, I would have to convert my American licence to a UK one at a cost of approximately £40,000. I was low on funds and had to decide what to do next.

I had two options – return to the UK and start my UK licence conversion or remain in the US and exercise the privilege of the J-1 visa.

The only concession the UK CAA gives is an exemption from Morse code. So, unless I could achieve 1,230 hours in 15 months, it might be better to get the British conversion on the way.

After a few days mulling it over, I decided to return to the UK. Having spent nine months in Scottsdale and made many friends, it was difficult to leave the sunshine of Arizona and head back to a London winter.

First, a UK Class 1 medical. It would be negligent to spend £80,000 only to find you couldn't pass the medical. Two schools were willing to accept me, the British Aerospace Flying College in Scotland and the Oxford Air Training School. I decided on the latter for ground training and basic flying, but Scotland for the expensive multi-engine portion.

The ground exams consist of 17 subjects split into two blocks, the navigation and technical subjects for the commercial licence. For the Airline Transport Pilot Licence (ATPL), the navigation subjects would be repeated at a more advanced level.

All 17 exams must be passed within three attempts and/or within a year of the first exam. The pass mark is 70 per cent for each exam and is negatively marked. Failure to complete all 17 exams in the required timeframe renders all previous passes null and void.

Money was running out, and I couldn't afford repeats. Each exam block costs thousands of pounds in boarding, tuition, and fees. If I was unable to make it through without repeats, I might have to give up.

I can still hear the words of my lecturers, 'If you don't know the answer, don't guess, leave it alone,' and 'RTFQ, RTFA' (read the full (fucking) question, read the (fucking) full answer).

Results for the Navigation exams would not be back for another month, but I got started on the technical subjects. Four weeks into the technical course, the navigation exam results were back. A brown envelope with the CAA stamp. My heart rate rose as I opened the envelope, convinced I had failed. I look at the individual subjects expecting to see fail. Next to each subject was the word PASS.

Next up the technical exams, and again I passed them all. Before I had received my results, I started the ATPL subjects. With all the ground exams passed, I could confront the practical part of the licence with a little more confidence.

On 9 May, I started flights at Kidlington Airport.

I celebrated my birthday as a UK basic commercial pilot. Next was the most critical and expensive portion of training, the UK instrument rating. A commercial licence is useless if you can only fly on sunny days.

Forty hours of twin-engine flying at £500 an hour. My finances were at breaking point; I simply could not fail. I thought about remortgaging the flat, but after Black Wednesday, I doubted there was any equity.

I was to be based at Adamton House for the next eight weeks. On 13 July, I started my UK instrument rating. My instructor was captain Geoff Sellick, a very relaxed and reserved man, one of the few non-military instructors. In my first briefing, he said, 'I know how expensive it is, so I will be working towards getting you through the course in 35 hours, just in case.'

In the coming weeks, we visited all the airports around Prestwick.

True to Geoff's word, I was ready for the CAA instrument rating test at 35 hours. My examiner was to be the legendary captain Dai Heather Hayes, call-sign Exam 11. I needed to know everything about Dai and be totally prepared. Geoff preached the 7Ps: Proper Prior Planning Prevents Piss Poor Performance.

On Tuesday 6 September, I walked down the corridor to the examiner's office and introduced myself. 'I am Ricardo Ellcock, your instrument rating candidate.' After discussing the tolerances, do's and don'ts, it was time for the routing. Prestwick to Belfast and on to Londonderry.

'Oh, my God. Londonderry. Where the fuck is that?' I have a couple of hours to book an aircraft, file a flight plan and know everything there is to know about the routing.

As I lined up on the runway and started the take-off, for the first time I was aware of the butterflies. I was turning the aircraft from left to right as I attempted to maintain track. Suddenly Dai reached across the cockpit and said, 'Young man, if you do not stop turning this aircraft, I shall vomit in your lap.'

Soon I am in contact with Aldergrove. 'Aldergrove approach, Exam 11'. One engine throttled back, and I started the approach. As I approached the decision height, the blinds remained in place; it was my cue to carry out the miss-approach procedure and start the turn toward Londonderry.

Once around the holding pattern, I started the approach, hoping it would soon be over. As I approached the minimum descent altitude, Dai asked for the position of the runway. I said, 'straight-ahead.' He said, 'I have control, and you can take the blinds down.' Dai would do the landing, and I could relax. It was over; all that remained was the signing of my licence.

I was still approximately three hours short of the approved course requirements. Perhaps the CAA would relax the requirement? The next morning, the CAA made their ruling. It is an approved course, and the 40 hours must be completed in full. Though disappointing, it allowed me to fly my guardian, Michael Clarke, around the highlands of Scotland. With all the exams and flight tests completed and some £80,000 spent, the pursuit of an airline job began.

After a short break, including getting married on 1 October, I started my research. It was not the ideal time to leave flight school as several airlines had gone bust since I started. Out of work and short on funds, my days were spent writing and sending letters. The return letters were polite but asked for experience on a modern flight guidance aircraft. The same old dilemma – you need the experience to get a job, but you need a job to get experience. Very soon, the letters become known as the FOL (fuck-off letters).

I was offered an interview by CTC Aviation, the same path several fellow flight school graduates had followed with success. The interview went well, and I felt optimistic. In another couple of weeks, a letter with the distinctive CTC stamp arrived. Surely this was the chance to start my aviation career. But as I opened the envelope, the word 'regret' stood out. I had missed out on the CTC programme.

With only Kate's salary to support us, money was short, and September was licence renewal, at the cost of £1,500.

By June 1995, rumours were circulating of LIAT requiring pilots. LIAT was founded in 1957 by Kittitian, Frank Delisle, to operate services between Montserrat and Antigua. After being bought by Court Line in 1971, LIAT was saved from bankruptcy by 11 Caribbean governments. Finally, on 21 July 1995, there was a message on the answering machine.

'Can you phone the Company Secretary of LIAT, Ms Finch'? They were offering an interview.

The catch: it was on 25 July.

Could I make it? I started phoning travel agents on Friday 22 July, managing to secure a flight landing in Antigua on Sunday evening. I knew of two fellow Combermerians flying for LIAT, captain Patrick Babb and senior first officer Derek Haynes *(Babb, Haynes and I met at Combermere in 1975, and they would eventually join me at Virgin Atlantic, the first three black pilots Virgin hired)*. If I was unable to get hold of either of them, accommodation would be expensive. However, the name Zoral Bartley came to mind, captain of the Leeward Islands under 19 team at the 1983 youth tournament in Jamaica. In the intervening years, he had also gone to flight school and acquired his licence but had opted to run the family business instead of taking up a flying career. Going forward, Zoral would be a godsend. I call him Mr Antigua; and time and again he would help me with transportation and accommodation. To think, 12 years earlier, we were enemies, and I was trying to knock his head off.

On 25 July, I start ground school for the DHC-6 Twin Otter. With interview and aircraft exams completed successfully, Trinidadian Richie Kangoo and I were the first two candidates to be selected for flight training. On 3 August, it was the first flight, up to the local training area, just south of Barbuda, Antigua's sister island. A new airline has started in Barbados, and several pilots had joined from LIAT, with Patrick Babb one of those. Senior first officer Derek Haynes was still with LIAT but now based in Barbados.

16 August 1995 was a very important date for me, as it was my first commercial flight. Flight number LI562, routing Antigua-Nevis-St Kitts-Nevis-Antigua-Canefield Dominica-Vigie St Lucia-Canefield Dominica-Guadeloupe-Antigua. The total flight time of this route is 5 hours and 24 minutes, and having checked in at 5am, I was back at the apartment around 3pm, totally exhausted.

After 40 hours of line training and ten flights, I was ready for my line check with chief pilot captain John Murray. He was a hard taskmaster who alternated between silence and screaming. His line checks were always the LI154, routing Antigua-Barbuda-Antigua-Guadeloupe-Canefield Dominica-Guadeloupe-Antigua, before the night flight Antigua-Montserrat-Antigua. The pilot under training was expected to fly the extremely challenging approaches into Canefield Dominica and Montserrat. Chief pilot Murray would apply as much pressure as possible, and during the return leg from Montserrat, he would become incapacitated. The trainee was expected to declare a simulated emergency, fly, land and taxi the aircraft before shutting the engines down, all without his help. At the end of this, you became a fully fledged Twin Otter first officer. After a few months on the Twin Otter, I moved to the Dash 8, big brother to the Twin Otter, a twin-engine turboprop-powered regional airliner with increased power, higher take-off and landing weight, higher cruise speed, and now pressurised, allowing for cruising altitudes up to 25,000 feet. This was a modern flight guidance aircraft. The Dash 8 routed as far north as the Dominican Republic and as far south as Georgetown, Guyana and Caracas, Venezuela. Learning to fly the Dash 8 in all weathers was a steep learning curve. All the while, I was still writing to airlines all over the world. I had spent some £80,000 on my licence and owed it to myself to fly the best equipment I can.

The dream of sitting in a British Airways or Virgin Atlantic 747 was within touching distance.

CHAPTER 20

IN COMMAND

At the beginning of January 1997, my wife, Kate, had phoned with good news. Virgin Atlantic had offered me an interview in February and I had got the job.

Fast forward eight years and it is 16 June 2005. After eight years as a first officer I am about to find out the route for my exam to become captain, but the rosters are late. The next morning, the brown envelope finally drops on the doormat. My pulse rate increases. The roster says LGW-BGI-LGW, with captain John Alexander on 6 July. The route to Barbados is excellent, but captain Alexander is considered one of the more difficult examiners to fly with, although we have always had a good working relationship. As a young second officer, at 38,000 feet over north-east Canada, captain Alexander and myself had experienced a total navigation failure. However, with careful co-operation, we managed to get the 747 to San Francisco safely.

Just then, the phone rings. It is Mark Fry. That Aussie accent is unmistakable, 'Hi mate, have you seen your roster? You've failed!' Typical Aussie humour!

The night of 5 July is spent contemplating all the things that can go wrong. The next morning I will be catching the train at 6.30am, arriving Gatwick at 7.30am as it spares me the early-morning M25. Flight departure is 10am; scheduled check-in 8.30am for pilots and 8am for cabin crew.

Two and half hours before departure, I have ample time to check for the *"gotchas"*. It will be another hour before captain Alexander arrives. I speak to the dispatcher. Is there anything unusual about today's flight? Hopefully, the engineers will tell me the aircraft is clear of all faults.

Captain Alexander arrives right on schedule; I have covered all the bases, and I am in a position to give him a complete brief. The scheduled flight time is precisely 7hr 40, the aircraft today is G-VAST, and he is happy with the weather.

All preparations completed, doors shut, we are rolling backwards at 9.53am, seven minutes ahead of schedule. We are airborne at 10.10am, and after an uneventful flight, we are at the gate at the Barbados Grantley Adams International Airport at 12.55pm. I feel it has not gone too badly, but it is not over until the parking brake is set back at London Gatwick. The crew check into the hotel; I buy everyone a drink before heading home for some of Mum's home cooking. She has asked me to bring my pilot shirts down to be washed.

A good night's sleep and I'm up for my pre-arranged breakfast with captain Alexander. I still have no real sense of how it is going. With England five hours ahead, the incoming aircraft should be on its way. A quick call to engineering will let me know if it left England with any issues. Later, a call to flight planning and handling will confirm routing, weather, cargo and fuel for the return leg. Finally, a call to ground staff here in Barbados will confirm crew wake-up calls and crew transport pick-up times. Remember the seven Ps.

Departure is at 17.20, but with all the groundwork I have done, I feel pretty composed. Captain Alexander is the operating pilot back to Gatwick, so he is preparing the aircraft before briefing me.

We push back at 17.16, flight VIR30; the aircraft again is G-VAST, the very first 747-400 I had ever flown, maybe a good omen. Captain Alexander has still not said a word about the check; but just before we reach the runway, he looks over and says: 'Rick, you have two basic jobs this sector; one is to raise the landing gear in a minute, the second is to lower it at the other end. If you can do those two things without fucking them up, you have passed. Now relax and enjoy the flight.'

We are at London Gatwick at 6.25am on 8 July; captain Alexander reaches into his flight bag, takes out a pair of captain's four bars, shakes me by the hand and says, 'Enjoy Command. Just remember when you look in the mirror, you will see a reflection of yourself. That is because from now on the buck will only ever stop with you.' Proudest day of my life. Captain of a Boeing 747-400.

Since sitting in the cockpit of an American fighter as a 12-year-old, I had wanted to fly aeroplanes. Today, 28 July 2005, is the day I can put to rest dad's assertion that black people do not fly aeroplanes. All the hard work has resulted in me taking command of a Boeing 747-400 for the first time, bound for Havana, Cuba.

After a restless night, playing every possible scenario over and over in my mind, I arrive in the crew room wearing my shiny new captain's jacket and four bars. My colleagues, senior first officer Darren Hinchey and senior first officer Keith Gracey, arrive. Keith is a fellow West Indian, from Jamaica, 90 miles from Cuba. As well as a source of knowledge about the local area, we can discuss the demise of West Indies cricket.

Two hours before departure, the briefing desk is covered in papers. Flight plans, weather, notams (notices to airmen), crew names, dangerous goods notices and take-off performance must all be studied. The pilot briefing must be interrupted to brief the cabin crew.

Three of us decide on fuel and discuss anything that might have a bearing on the safety of the flight. Usually, at this stage, we spin a toss to determine who will fly the aeroplane outbound and who will bring it back. Today, as I'm a rookie captain, I must do both landings.

Boarding must start by T minus 55. The scheduled departure time (T) is 10am. Engineers are still on board; firstly, I must look at the tech log to ensure there are no show-stoppers, and then check the PA system. With the aircraft given the all-clear, the two operating pilots can get on and prepare the flight deck, whilst the third pilot can do the walk around.

With boarding under way, a gentle peace descends on the flight deck. It's time for the Flight Management System (FMS) to be programmed, which requires maximum concentration.

T minus 40 and it's time to calculate the final fuel for the trip. The 747-400, on average burns approximately ten tonnes of fuel an hour, and with a flight time of nine hours the fuel figure should be around 90 tonnes.

The FMS has been fully programmed. It is Darren's cue to ask for take-off clearance. 'Virgin 63, you are cleared to Havana via the Southampton 2 Foxtrot, maintain 6000 and Squawk 2663.' I must now brief the other two pilots on my departure plans and any "gotchas" we might encounter.

T minus 10. Time to let the passengers know this is not the Mary Celeste.

Good morning, ladies and gentlemen; welcome aboard this Boeing 747-400 aircraft, Virgin 63, bound for Havana, Cuba. My name is Ricky Ellcock, the captain. Here on the flight deck with myself are senior first officer Darren Hinchey and senior first officer Keith

167

Gracey; three of us, along with the 15 members of the cabin crew, are here, primarily for your safety but also to ensure your trip is as comfortable as possible. Today we are departing off the westerly runway, and our routing takes us along the south coast of England down to Lands' End, where we will start our Atlantic crossing. That will take us south of the Azores, overhead Bermuda, south of Miami, across the Bahamas, south of Hispaniola, and along the north coast of Cuba out to Havana on the northern tip. Flight time is 9 hours, and we have an initial cruising altitude of 34,000 feet. Excellent weather forecast along the route, but if you are seated, please keep your seat belts fastened as we might encounter unforecast turbulence at these altitudes. I know some of you will try and get some rest, so I will not bother you any further. I will now leave you in the capable hands of the cabin crew, and I will speak to you again about 30 minutes before landing in Havana. In the meantime, sit back, relax and enjoy the flight.

As I finish the PA, the engineer arrives with the tech log and fuel chit for signature. The flight service manager asks all ground staff to leave the aircraft. I ask Darren to get a call in for push and start. As the last door closes, the call comes from air traffic control, 'Virgin 63 cleared to push and start, face west.' 'Ground flight deck, can I have your checks?' The tug driver replies, 'All equipment cleared, pin inserted, and you are cleared to pressurise.' I ask Darren for the before start checks.

'Ground, flight deck,' I call.

The tug driver replies,

'Capt. Ground standing by.'

'Ground, we are cleared to push and start, facing west, park brake set.'

'Capt. Release brakes.'

'Brakes released.'

'Ok, rolling, cleared to start. Can you give us an off-time?'

'Off at 0858 UTC, starting. 4, 3, 2, 1.'

The last engine starts. 'Ground, flight deck, four good starts; thanks for all the help, and enjoy the rest of your day.' 'Thanks, captain; safe flight.' I ask for flaps twenty and the after-start checks.

Without prompting, Darren says, 'Ground Virgin 63 requesting taxi.' 'Virgin 63, cleared taxi, Juliett, Papa, hold Alpha 2.' 'Brakes released, taxi lights on.' With a little power, the 747 creeps forward along the taxiway toward the holding point Alpha 2.

Holding Alpha 2; all take-off checks completed. I have a moment to reflect on my life. I feel so fortunate to have had two incredible careers. People pay a lot of money to do both of my careers as hobbies. If you ask most little boys what they want to do when they are older, I suspect the vast majority of them would say professional sportsman or pilot. I have managed to do both, and for that, I feel eternally privileged, grateful and blessed.

Just then, the call comes, 'Virgin 63 cleared take-off runway 26 Left.' I advance the thrust levers, and with the aircraft lined up, I press the take off and go around switches. The thrust levers automatically advance to the correct power setting. As the speeds build, Darren calls 80kts. Moments later, he calls V1. I take my hands off the thrust levers as this is the speed the decision is made to go flying. Moments later, he calls rotate, and I gently pull back on the control column. All 335 tonnes of the Jumbo climb into the skies. It has happened; I'm a captain of a Jumbo jet. The first black captain Virgin Atlantic has employed. My only regret is that neither Dad nor Alan Duff are alive to witness it.

CHAPTER 21

NEAR DEATH

I have now been in command of a Jumbo jet for nine years. Departed Barbados at 6.58pm on 13 February 2014, flight VIR30, Barbados to London Gatwick, cruising at 37,000 feet, estimating arrival at London Gatwick at 6.30am on Valentine's Day. A cabin crew arrives on the flight deck with a note:

Hi, Ricky; it is your mates, Smudge Smith and Alan Wells, sitting down the back; we would love to see the cockpit.

I send a return message, saying I am unable to show them the cockpit while airborne due to security measures, but I will have them brought up as soon as we are parked. Soon after parking, a cabin crew arrives on the flight deck with my former cricket adversaries. "Smudge" wants to know all about the inner workings of the 747-400. Alan is concerned the college he coaches have offered a scholarship to Shamar Springer, a talented cricketer at, Combermere. The school's head coach, Roddy Estwick, has turned down the offer. However, he feels with me having received a scholarship myself and being a Combermere old boy and a former cricket colleague of Roddy, I might have some leverage. I promise to help if I can. Before leaving the flight deck, Smudge shakes my hand, 'Rick, I would like to apologise for my behaviour back in our playing days. I was a wanker.'

As they disappear into the terminal, I gather my belongings as the crew bus will be waiting. I walk along the upper deck of the 747-400 and start to descend the stairs. Then, disaster strikes.

I miss my step and fall to the bottom of the stairs. I look up at the engineers chuckling, 'The bar isn't even open yet!' Very funny. As I walk away, it doesn't feel so funny. I fall to the ground again. And again. My right leg is unable to bear my weight. With my right knee swelling, the paramedics are called and an ambulance is required.

The nearest hospital is the East Surrey in Redhill. A junior doctor can't understand why I can move my toes but not my leg. With the x-rays back, she is baffled further; there are no broken bones, but I can't move my leg. She summons an A&E doctor, who recognises a quadricep tear and advises corrective surgery.

After four days awaiting a theatre slot, I'm finally seen by an Indian doctor with a love of cricket. He promises to fit me in the following day. I spend a further two weeks in hospital before being plastered from groin to toes and discharged. Unable to drive or fit into an ordinary car, I ask my department management for transport from the hospital to home, two hours away. The request is denied. It will take an email from my lawyer to the CEO of Virgin Atlantic for the company to make a U-turn.

Being adept at rehab, I take it upon myself to regain full fitness. On 11 August 2014, I step back into the 747-400 simulator. The CAA medical department wants me to undertake a proving flight. I must be able to maintain rudder pressure with my right leg for a period of time. With the proving flight successful, I go on to command the Jumbo until 2 June 2015. VIR78, Barbados to Manchester, aircraft G-VGAL, my last 747-400 flight. I pull into the gate at Manchester airport, set the parking brake, and wish the "Queen of the Skies" a fond farewell.

My new aircraft is the 787-900, "The Dreamliner". After weeks of learning the systems, standard operating procedures, safety procedures, and equipment, I start simulator training on 30 October at the Boeing Flight Training Centre in Crawley. After eight four-hour simulator sessions, I undertake my first 787 flight, the VIR250, to Shanghai on 27 November. With line training completed successfully, I settle down to learning and improving my operation of the Dreamliner.

However, I begin to have bouts of sinusitis. Usually, a course of antibiotics and rest sees me back airborne. For most of my life, I have been free of illness; lots of sporting injuries but not illnesses. But now, I'm seeing the doctor continuously for any number of aches and pains. Now over 50, perhaps some of these aches are the result of playing professional cricket from the age of 16. Suddenly I'm waking some mornings with headaches and neck pain, which are producing numbness in my right hand and fingers. My doctor thinks I might be sleeping in a bad position.

I'm beginning to feel my depression has returned.

In September 2017, I apply to the University of Westminster and am accepted on the Air Transport Planning and Management MSc course. I aim to finish in January 2019. However, as I will be doing this while working full-time, I must be totally focused.

171

I continue to experience periodic headaches, neck pain, occasional finger numbness, vertigo, and, most worrying, significant deterioration of my eyesight. My optician is unconcerned as, up to this stage, he had felt I was blessed not to have suffered the same deterioration as most people after age 40. Apart from my vanity and ego, my concern is that my right eye is deteriorating faster than the left. Without my newly prescribed glasses, I'm having to see long-distance with my left eye and read with my right eye. The optician assures me that most people have variances in vision between their eyes.

The Dreamliner is sold to airlines as an aircraft with a lower cabin altitude than older models. For most passengers, a long flight is followed by some combination of symptoms that include headaches, lack of appetite, lack of energy, nausea, and sleeplessness. These symptoms are usually known as jetlag, but they are the same symptoms attributed to acute mountain sickness due to exposure to altitudes above 6,500 feet. The Dreamliner maintains a cabin altitude below 6,000 feet and is therefore meant to alleviate these symptoms. Yet after each of my flights, I'm experiencing them, as well as neck pain, right-side numbness, lack of concentration and memory lapses. Perhaps the workload of the MSc course and full-time flying is taking its toll.

The November 2018 roster is busy. I have eight weeks before my thesis deadline on 7 January, with my final MSc exam the next day. The roster comprises three days of leave, three flights – Los Angeles, Boston and San Francisco – two days of simulator training, two days of ground training, one e-learning training day, and ten days clear of duty. I have booked leave between 1 and 23 of January. I plan to spend two weeks on the beach in Barbados after my final exam.

This year I will spend Christmas in England, putting the final touches to my thesis and revising for my final MSc exam. It is a real disappointment to be away from the family on Christmas Day. Every Christmas since I was a kid, my mum has hosted upwards of 30 family members and friends for Christmas lunch. It is a boisterous affair but an opportunity to see friends and family I have not seen throughout the year. I will try to call my mum to get a bit of the atmosphere.

My three days off begin with a thumping headache requiring a prescription from my GP for painkillers. I do not feel at all well, but with the medication, I'm soon up and about. I'm reluctant to call in sick, especially this close to Christmas, as the company always suspect pilots are skiving.

18 December, London Heathrow to Los Angeles. Return leg three days later. We arrive at LAX at 1.35pm, an hour and 20 minutes before departure. Having checked my bags in, I head to the gate. Boarding complete, doors closed, we are rolling backwards at 2.49pm, local LAX time. I'm the flying pilot with co-pilot senior first officer Seamus Duff. The crew relief pilot on this leg is senior first officer Paul Humphrey. Being relief pilot, Paul will sit in the jump-seat for take-off, and as we climb through 10,000 feet, he will proceed to the inflight crew rest area, which consists of two beds and a chair in an area positioned in the roof of the aircraft, above the upper-class cabin. Relief pilots use this area to read, watch movies and sleep during long flights. With a flight time of approximately 10 hours, the three of us will each get three hours of crew rest, and we all will be back in the cockpit an hour before landing.

By the time I get into crew rest, I have a thumping headache, my neck pain has returned, and my co-ordination is deteriorating. I feel terrible, but hopefully, three hours in the bunk will cure this. Unable to sleep straight away, I attempt a crossword. Unable to do that, I try the sudoku but that is even less successful. Eventually, I drop off to sleep. I am soon awake, disorientated and convinced that I have overslept and that we have landed with me not on the flight deck. As I rush to get dressed, I'm unable to button my trousers or shirt. I sit on the crew rest seat and slow my actions down. But try as I may I'm unable to fasten my trousers or shirt. I cannot even lace my shoes. I have lost all co-ordination.

My left hand seems better than the right, but overall, I'm unable to carry out simple actions. In this state, it would be unwise and unsafe to try to land the aircraft. I need to see a doctor, but first I need to hand over command of the aircraft. I ask the flight service manager to put out a call for a doctor and to ask senior first officer Seamus Duff to meet me in the forward galley. Seamus is the non-handling pilot on this sector and is seated in the right-hand seat. The chain of command passes first to the occupant of the right-hand seat and then to the relief pilot. I explain that I feel incapable of safely landing the aircraft. With less than an hour to touch-down, I ask him to declare a mayday. It is repeated three times and guarantees priority handling by air traffic control, as well as putting medical and fire services on standby.

With command handed over, two LA-based doctors, father and son, on a fishing trip to Scotland, arrive. I sit on the jump seat for my examination, which includes eye movements, touching my nose, squeezing their fingers with both hands, followed by blood pressure, heart-rate, and blood sugar tests. As we land, I can see the emergency services out of the window. The airport paramedics repeat the checks and are unable to identify a cause, so it is decided a visit to hospital is the best course of action. Hillingdon Hospital in Uxbridge is 15 minutes away. I have no movement in my right leg, and I am unable to control my bladder. During the short trip, the ambulance driver has to stop twice so I can relieve myself.

At the hospital, the in-house doctor is baffled.

'I don't believe you have had a stroke, but the symptoms seem to be neurological, so I'm going to send you to the neurological department to see a specialist.'

I set off as directed but cannot find the department; I am at my wit's end. A young doctor, noticing my confusion, asks if he can help. I show him the specialist's request and he takes me to the right department.

There, the sixth set of checks is carried out. With no conclusion, I'm in a cubicle awaiting a CT scan. Soon Lisa, a long-time friend stationed at Heathrow, arrives and we await the scan together. The procedure takes 30 minutes, and I begin the torturous walk back, at which point I sense the mood of the doctors and nurses has changed. They are talking in hushed tones. I hear a nurse ask for an ambulance. She says, 'It's an emergency, I need a blue light.' I ask Lisa to get a little closer and find out if it is for me. As she approaches, the conversation stops. I'm convinced my condition is terminal. My thoughts are of brain tumours, cancer, or a stroke. I'm scared. I send Lisa back to ask what is going on. She returns with the message that a doctor will soon be over. My heart is pounding as the same doctor who ordered the CT scan parts the curtain and stands in front of me.

'Have you been involved in a car accident recently?'

'No.'

'What about falling off a ladder?'

'No.'

'Falling down stairs?'

'Yes, about four years ago.'

'No, recently.'

'No.'

'Do you remember banging your head recently?'

'No.'

'You have a subdural haematoma, caused by a traumatic brain injury.'

I'm relieved. I would get a haematoma under the nail of my left big toe, caused by it slamming into the front of my cricket boot every year during my cricket career. The physio would drill a hole in the nail, release the blood, and I would be back on the field.

'Ok, I thought it was going to be serious. I'll go home, get some sleep and get it sorted tomorrow.'

'You will not be going home; it will kill you if we don't operate today.'

Oh!

I'm sent to St Mary's Hospital, where I'm wheeled into what looks like a theatre. I'm trying to count the number of people in the room. With all the different types and colours of uniforms, I cannot make any sense of what is going on.

'Who is in charge?' I ask.

I'm told no one is in charge; everyone carries out their job.

'Who is the boss, then?'

'There is no boss.'

'Who is the captain?'

Sensing my frustration, a gentleman of Iraqi or Iranian descent steps forward.

'Captain, I will be the operating surgeon.'

'Ok, you are the commander.'

'Captain, you have a left-sided subdural haematoma, and there are two methods of clearing it. We can do a craniotomy, where we temporarily remove a section of the skull so I can access and remove the haematoma. Or we can drill a small hole into the skull, and insert a tube through it to help drain the haematoma. I would suggest a craniotomy as it gives me the option of reopening it in the case of a rebleed.'

175

I make an illegible scribble on the operation permission form. I give my next of kin as my son Isaac, my ex-wife Kate, and Mum. It is three days before Christmas, and I leave instructions not to inform my next of kin unless I die.

I wake on the trauma ward, on the eighth floor of St Mary's, early in the morning on 22 December. My head is sore from the surgery, but the headache and stiff neck have gone. The surgeon will be doing his rounds around 10am. I now have 16 days to submit my thesis, so I need to be on my feet ASAP. Early morning, and my surgeon is in. He feels the operation went well but wants me to be under observation for a week. He will administer a course of anti-seizure medication. He says this is prudent as a seizure will have dire consequences for my job. I reckon I can get some studying done over the next week while I'm stuck here.

Christmas morning, I'm up early. I'm now free to move around and have a shower. No one apart from Lisa knows I'm here. I want it this way as I don't want to spoil anyone's Christmas. I spend the morning studying before lunch is served. It is fair to say, a disappointment – three slices of turkey, two slices of white toast, and some brown Brussels sprouts. One of my fellow patients wheels himself to my bedside to suggest the meal cost them 70p.

I fire off my Christmas calls to unsuspecting friends in England. The big one will be to my mum. Barbados is four hours behind, so at around 6pm in the UK will be when the family is sitting down for lunch. I usually do video calls but will refrain from that this time for obvious reasons. All the family is there and in good spirits and I am happy everyone is enjoying their Christmas. Kate and Isaac are spending theirs with her mum in Stoke-on-Trent. I have decided to tell them on Boxing Day.

My discharge is scheduled for 27 December. I will be staying with Kate and Isaac in Dollis Hill, a couple of miles from St Mary's. My neurosurgeon believes it would be unwise to attempt an exam on 8 January, one day after submitting my thesis. My next ten days are spent in the Jawi Communication internet café on Willesden High Road. My research into optimising flight crew rostering to avoid fatigue has been completed. However, my findings must be typed, formatted, and sent to be printed and submitted to the University of Westminster before midnight on 7 January. I will then sit my final exam.

As I approach 7 January, the long days and nights in the internet café putting the final touches to my thesis are taking their toll. My headaches, stiff neck, and double vision are back. My lack of sleep is playing havoc with my co-ordination and my bladder is again proving troublesome. I'm anxiously anticipating walking out of my final exam. On the morning of 6 January, I'm finally happy with my thesis. I send an electronic version to the university well ahead of the submission deadline and another to the printers.

It is a relief to have beaten the deadline. With the thesis completed and submitted, I take to my bed. I plan to revise tomorrow before travelling to Marylebone for my final exam. However, I wake in the early hours of the morning with a severe headache, and I'm unable to hold my phone in my right hand. I clumsily make breakfast and sit at the dining room table surrounded by my books. I'm unable to write or concentrate, and I'm getting dizzy spells. I need to see a doctor. I phone for an Uber and ask to be taken to A&E at St Mary's for yet another triage. When they hear about my brain operation just two weeks ago, I'm prioritised to be seen by a neurosurgeon. I am rushed to the scanning department, and another CT scan is carried out. The brain bleed is back, and I'm admitted to the major trauma ward again. Another brain operation to evacuate the blood is needed. It is scheduled for later that evening. No one knows I'm back in hospital. I must get the news to my son, but continue to keep it from my mum.

With the operation carried out, I'm back in the trauma ward in the early hours of 8 January. I ask the doctor if there is any chance of a lift to Westminster, a short distance from St Mary's. My exam is scheduled for 9.30am. He is not sure if I'm joking or if my cognitive function has been impaired. I'm actually not sure myself.

I am discharged for the second time on 12 January, on this occasion without the same concern about seizures. After a restless night, I'm up early. The headache is back. It can't be another bleed. It must be the feathers in the pillow. As a kid, I was allergic to feathers. I feel pretty rotten, but the pain seems to subside with paracetamol.

Each morning, the headache is back. Am I imagining my hand shaking? My clumsiness? Perhaps the panic attacks are back?

It surely can't be another brain bleed...

Wednesday, 16 January. Kate is away working in Los Angeles, and Isaac is at his job in the city. It has been four days since my discharge. I'm again awake with a headache and the shakes, but the paracetamol is not working. I call an Uber and return to A&E at St Mary's. I'm rushed through triage and again prioritised to see a neurosurgeon. On this occasion, I see two. They run through the co-ordination test and seem satisfied with the results. I wonder out loud if it is worth me getting another scan. But they remind me, it is only a week since the operation. I leave the hospital feeling patronised but relieved the doctors believe nothing is seriously wrong.

On the morning of 17 January, the headache is still there, but I'm determined to return to my house in Frimley in Surrey. I arrive after the long train journey – Jubilee line from Dollis Hill to Waterloo, then Southwestern line from Waterloo to Ascot and Frimley, and then the short walk to Bicknell Road. The headache is now unbearable, so I lie on the sofa in the sitting room and fall asleep.

The next thing I know I am being woken by a paramedic.

He is asking me rapid-fire questions. Where are you? What is your name? Where do you work? Where were you born? What car do you drive? I answer them all, but he says my speech is slurred, and I need to go to the A&E department at Frimley Park Hospital. My girlfriend Denise, who had been away on holiday, had called the ambulance because of my confusion, slurred and gibberish speech. This is my third ambulance ride and fourth visit to A&E in three weeks.

I'm taken through yet another triage, and with my recent history, it is decided I should have another CT scan, which is then sent to St Mary's for an opinion.

Moments later, the doctor returns to advise, 'St Mary's neuro department believe the CT scans are normal for this stage of brain surgery recovery. However, I am not comfortable with that diagnosis and would like to keep you in overnight for observation.'

As the night progresses, my speech becomes more laboured. I'm confused and disorientated. Soon I'm unable to text, and when Kate phones from Los Angeles, I'm aware of her questions but unable to speak. I'm deteriorating rapidly. During the early hours of the morning on 18 January, the decision is made to take me back to St Mary's. I'm being stretchered along the hallway and just before entering the ambulance, I'm aware of a cold draft. As I'm being buckled in, my body begins shaking uncontrollably and my eyes rolling to the right. My body is out of control. I can hear the two ambulance drivers shouting, 'What is happening?' 'Hold him!' 'Protect his head!'

Almost as soon as it has started, it is over, and I have regained control of my body. The ambulance drivers decide they are not equipped to deal with seizures en route to St Mary's, and I am returned to the neurological team. I am given 500mg of Keppra and a nurse with further drugs accompanies the ambulance crew to St Mary's. A CT scan confirms a rebleed, and a third operation is carried out to evacuate the re-accumulating of the left-sided subdural haematoma. Tonic-clonic seizures start, and I'm administered Phenytoin. With my condition taking a turn for the worse, the decision is made to tell my mum. I had sworn everyone to secrecy in the hope of shielding my Barbados family from this situation. My mum and brother decide to travel to England and will arrive on 22 January.

Despite being on Phenytoin, the seizures are difficult to control. I suffer from right-sided jaw clenching, becoming tonic-clonic, followed by a long postictal phase with expressive dysphasia. I'm now also given the seizure drug Levetiracetam. On the morning of 22 January, I'm up early in preparation for my family arriving. My nearest bathroom in the major trauma ward is occupied, so I have to walk to the next available bathroom. I walk in, lock the bathroom door, and get undressed. As I turn the shower on, I am aware of a very peculiar feeling. I know I have to lie down on the floor or I will fall over. I totally lose control of my body. I cannot speak or move, but my body is shaking uncontrollably. I can hear and I can see. I am aware that the shower is still running and I am able to thank the Lord I'm not in a bath. I am also able to tell myself to be patient; it will be over soon. I think around ten minutes have gone by, and I'm still violently seizing. Then, my prayers are answered – someone is trying to get in. But the door is locked! I hear them walk away. Another 10 minutes pass by. Another pull at the door. They walk away, too. More people come to the door. And all of them walk away again. I'm convinced I will die in this bathroom unless I can somehow unlock the door.

I decide to roll towards it. A heave and I'm now lying face down on the wet bathroom floor. I have to get myself face up. Another heave and I manage it. That has taken all my strength, but I'm now closer to the door. I reckon two or three more heaves will put me within touching distance. I can still hear the odd person trying the door. A few more heaves, and I'm lying at the base of the door. The seizure seems to be getting worse, and I have no strength left. I have to release the lock. One final heave, and the door flies open. Suddenly I'm half in the corridor. I can see nurses standing around. One of them turns and looks at me, lying naked on the floor. She runs over and stops my head from banging on the floor. Another, in a hijab, is shouting, 'He is biting his tongue!' while another is asking someone to get the doctor.

A 53-year-old known patient was in the toilet when he was found on the floor seizing. The patient was lying on his back, the R side of the face twitching. The patient was given 2mg of Lorazepam, seemed to come around but did not. I was called and could only pick up the bleep after finishing inserting an ICP monitor. By then, the patient had been seizing continuously for about 12 mins. I advised to give him another 2mg of Lorazepam, get medical team and likely the anaesthetic team involved while I make my way to the ward for resus. On my arrival patient was lying on the floor on his back, head turned to the left, eye deviation to the left, right arm and face twitching, moving his legs spontaneously, though eyes open but not reacting. As the patient was on therapeutical Phenytoin dose, I decided with med reg not to give him more. The seizure was to go on for a further 45 minutes; the anaesthetic team then intubated the patient.

It is 25 January. "Bohemian Rhapsody" by Queen is playing. There are several people around the bed, including Mum, looking devastated. The conversation among the doctors is about getting the seizures to stop long enough to allow an MRI scan. Eventually, they decide to risk it.

MRI complete, I'm wheeled back to the ward. Immediately, a neurosurgeon arrives.

'Rick, we have found the problem and must return to surgery.'

I'm exhausted, confused and want this over. 'Four weeks of CT scans, a single MRI, and you have found the problem?' My thoughts: I could not give a flying fuck. Why the fuck did you not do an MRI three operations ago? I have had enough.

The MRI scan has shown an area of suspected infection; there is also brain herniation through the fenestrated membrane, and a mid-line shift which is likely to cause brain irritation, resulting in severe seizure activity despite the administration of numerous anti-epileptic medications. The neurosurgeon is recommending an extension of the existing craniotomy, a resection of the membrane, a wash-out of any infection with sample for histopathology, the excision of subdural membranes, drainage of subdural and subdural wash-out.

The operation will be carried out in the next couple of hours. However, before he disappears to prepare for the operation, Kate asks him one further question:

'Are you the best at carrying out this type of operation?'

'I don't know if I'm the best, but I have carried out numerous operations of this type.'

Isaac is incensed with his mum; thinking it disrespectful to ask a surgeon such a question. Kate's answer, 'Rick would want me to ask.'

Fucking right, I would! To my mind, these guys have already made three almighty fuck-ups.

The operation is complete, and I am awake in the ICU, unable to speak and paralysed down my right side. My seizures are continuing. I'm afraid and paranoid that my medication is incorrect. I'm frustrated because I cannot tell my nurse about my fears. He is frustrated because he cannot understand my needs. 'Do you want a drink?' 'Are you hungry?' 'Do you want the loo?' 'Can you draw what you want?' I'm unable to do that because of my right-sided paralysis. 'If I write the alphabet, can you point the letters out?' I can't. I'm totally frustrated, unable to speak. I lie on the bed and begin to cry.

I wish I was dead. I wish there was a plug I could pull and end it all.

Just as I reach rock bottom, Kate appears from behind the curtain. 'How are you doing, Rick?' I make several excitable, totally unrecognisable noises. She looks me in the eye and says to the nurse, 'I think he is worried about his medication.' How the fuck did she do that? All day, in between seizures, I have been trying to tell my ICU nurse to ensure my anti-seizure medication is correct. I cannot speak, and he cannot understand my gestures, but within a minute of looking me in the eye, Kate knows the question I want to ask. I look at her in total amazement, thinking to myself, 'You must be fucking psychic!'

Over the next few days, my speech gradually returns, but my right-side paralysis continues. Even though I continue to have seizures, they are becoming less frequent and of shorter duration. A subsequent MRI has shown a subdural infection. The professor believes this might be the result of skin bacteria introduced during the operation. The drugs Cef and Linezolid are introduced.

On 28 January, I am transferred to Charing Cross Hospital. I'm still experiencing seizures in my right hand. Nurse Pauline is incredibly kind. She sits on the edge of my bed and cradles my head for the duration of each seizure. She reassures me the seizures will soon be over.

2 February. It has been a couple of days since my last seizure, and the decision has been made to move me to a private room to begin my rehab.

My mum has now been in England since 22 January and has travelled to each hospital for the duration of visiting hours. These are now extended from 10am to 10pm. Day after day, she walks into the room at 10am, having caught the Jubilee line from Dollis Hill to Green Park, changed to the Piccadilly line to Hammersmith and walked along the Fulham Palace Road. At 10pm, she does it all in reverse.

My rehab begins in earnest. The therapist is seriously concerned about my cognitive function, though I can still remember all my PINs, phone numbers, passwords, and addresses. I'm more concerned about my slurred speech and lack of movement in my right-hand. It is frustrating to do the memory and pictorial games while unable to button my shirt, use a knife and fork, or brush my teeth. Soon enough, my panic attacks are back. I'm afraid to have any doors closed, and despite requesting they be kept open, the nurses continue to close them. Finally, when one nurse can't draw blood, and another does not know how to use the blood glucose machine, I have had enough of the fuck-ups and want to return to Pauline on the public ward. The brain infection is proving stubborn, and I'm experiencing severe night sweats. The seizures seem to be a thing of the past, and the doctors are thinking of discharging me, but with a PIC line so intravenous antibiotics can be administered at home by community nurses.

12 February 2019 is discharge day. Today is the first time I have managed to fit all the coasters on the tree mug using my right hand

alone. For two weeks, this simple task to stimulate dexterity and movement has proved elusive. Tying my shoelaces and zipping my jacket for the journey home shows my progress.

I still have a long way to go, but after weeks of trauma and drama, I can see light at the end of the tunnel.

For the next six weeks, community nurses will visit me twice daily to administer intravenous antibiotics. In addition, I will travel every Monday morning to the tropical disease clinic at Charing Cross Hospital, and I'm now taking 29 tablets daily. My next appointment with the surgeon is in two months.

Two months pass, and my mum has felt confident enough to return to Barbados. My right hand is still not back to normal, but the PIC line has been removed. My surgeon is happy with the latest MRI, and with no seizure activity, he has cut my medication in half. He is happy for me to start light exercise, but I must stay away from heights, uninhabited areas, and water. My next appointment will be in eight weeks.

Two months later, it is June, and I'm still seizure-free. Although my right hand has improved, intricate movements are still an issue. However, my panic attacks are back in full force. Closed doors scare me, and I'm unable to have a bath. Every itch or muscle twitch sends me into major panic, fearful of a seizure attack. There are further improvements in the latest MRI scans, and the surgeon is happy to further reduce the anti-seizure medication. He wants to see me again in another eight weeks. I use my previous experience of injury rehab to build myself a training programme, and over the next eight weeks, I progress from walking to cycling to running. A large portion of my day is spent in the gym. During this period, my anti-seizure medication is reduced to a single tablet, taken twice daily. My surgeon is in favour of stopping the medication altogether, but these last two tablets are my comfort blanket. I have asked if hospital admission would be possible during final medication withdrawal.

20 August is my final scheduled MRI and EEG.

The ventricles are of normal size and configuration. The craniocervical junction is normal. There are no intra-axial abnormalities seen within the brainstem or cerebellum. There is no evidence of any intra-axial haemorrhage on the gradient echo sequence. Haemosiderin is noted in the subdural compartment on the gradient echo sequence as expected, but there is no evidence of any residual subdural haematoma. There was slight effacement to the sulci on the left hemisphere at the site of the previous subdural, which is of uncertain significance. There are no other abnormalities.

The EEG is not entirely normal but reveals episodic slow-wave (delta/theta) thus over the left hemisphere maximal temporary, likely to affect a degree of ipsilateral nonspecific cerebral dysfunction post-subdural haematoma.

There are, however, no overt epileptiform features noted to suggest a seizure disorder. Hyperventilation and photic stimulation were unremarkable.

With my anti-seizure medication finally at an end and still seizure-free, my final appointment with the surgeon is on 3 September 2019. The conclusion is that the fall down the stairs of the 747 Jumbo in 2014 had produced a chronic bleed which, over the years, had formed a membrane which had eventually grown large enough to shift and put pressure on my brain. Nevertheless, the surgeon is happy my medical issues have been resolved, and I can now continue my drive to fly a 787 again.

Having been signed off by the surgeon, it is now up to my dentist to repair all the cracked teeth on the right side of my mouth caused by the numerous seizures. I have decided to spend the winter in Barbados. I will train as hard as I possibly can. I'm now up to running seven miles, five days a week. My training is done in the midday sun, wearing black bin liners and without drinking any water. I aim to push my body to the very limit. It is my way of stress-testing my brain to see if I can provoke a reaction.

Christmas 2019, all the family gathered at my mum's house in Redman's Village, St Thomas. A year ago, I was lying in the trauma ward at St Mary's. I had deliberately not told anyone so as not to ruin the family Christmas. Mum, or "Pope" as she is known throughout the village and by all the family, has been cooking all night and is so happy to have everyone healthy and at home enjoying Christmas.

As the new year arrives, there is news of a new virus spreading across the world. With my health issues, I feel the best course of action is to return to London. I depart Barbados on the VIR30 on 4 February 2020, and settle back into the cold, dark, wet days in England.

On 9 February around 10am, I notice a couple of missed calls from my cousin, Stacey, in Barbados. They are four hours behind and it's perhaps a little too early to call back. I will return the call later. Just then, the phone rings. It is Stacey.

'Rick, the Pope has been found unresponsive.'

'What do you mean? What the fuck does that mean! I spoke to her yesterday.'

I cannot believe it. This time a year ago, my mum was negotiating the tube to visit me at Charing Cross Hospital. She had been to London in November to attend my MSc graduation, and now, three days short of the first anniversary of my discharge from the hospital, she is dead.

I feel so helpless. How can life be so fucking cruel?

* * *

Three years later...

I am awake at 6am; it is 84 degrees, and there is not a cloud in the sky. I make my way past the 18th green and clubhouse of the Green Monkey championship golf course at the Sandy Lane Hotel. I am a mile from the Platinum coast; my destination is the turquoise water of the Caribbean sea. My morning run will terminate on the beach in front of the Surf Side beach bar, where I will swim, followed by a tropical breakfast of fruit and Bajan coffee. My health issues, mental and physical, are behind me. I am very happy and can't wait for the next chapter.

APPENDIX

BIAS, PREJUDICE AND RACISM

Everson McDonald Ellcock. "Evie" was born on 30 September 1937, approximately 100 years after emancipation. In the same year, spontaneous riots erupted in Barbados, a rebellion against the white minority holding total economic and political power. The British colonialists, including marines and sailors from HMS Apollo, moved with brutal force to end the uprising, resulting in the death of 14 Barbadians and the wounding of 47 others.

The name Ellcock began with the ancient Anglo-Saxon tribes, first found in Derbyshire and Cambridgeshire, where the Hundredorum Rolls of 1273 listed Alcok de Stonys and John Alcoc. Alcok, Alcoc, Elcock and Ellcock are variations of the name.

Several Ellcocks landed in the Caribbean during the 17th and 18th centuries.

My family name is believed to come from one such arrival, Mr Reynold Alleyne Ellcock, owner of approximately 460 slaves in the Rock Hall area, then part of the Mount Wilton Plantation in St Thomas, Barbados. In his 1820 will, he left five pounds sterling to each of his adult slaves. Unfortunately, when news of the will leaked out, his throat was slashed by his valet. He was buried at St Thomas parish church on 4 October 1821. Mr Reynold Alleyne Ellcock's estate was awarded compensation under the Slave Compensation Act 1837 of approximately £10,000 for his slaves, the equivalent of £7.5 million today.

* * *

Marian Ione Ellcock (née Husbands). "Pope" was born on 16 June 1946. The name Husbands was a name for peasant farmers. It was originally derived from the Old English "husband", which meant one who tills the soil. The name was first found in Bedfordshire (Bedanfordscir), formerly part of the Anglo-Saxon Kingdom of Mercia, where lands were granted to them by Duke William for their assistance at the battle of Hastings in 1066. Several variations of spelling exist and include Husbands, Husbants, and Husborne. It is believed Mum's name comes from Evans Henry Husbands, who arrived in Barbados in 1781.

With slaves taking the names of their owners. It is easy to connect the names Ellcock and Husbands to the Atlantic slave trade.

Even after slavery, British colonisation left a legacy in Barbados of entitlement and privilege for a small minority, and a lack of opportunity for the larger majority. That majority was invariably black, with entitlement and privilege based on skin shading from white through red, brown and finally black. In effect, an apartheid, caste and class system existed and, to a lesser extent, remains in place today.

My mother and father suffered under this system, leaving school early to help support their families. Dad would say, 'I got a trade at 13 years old', meaning he left school and became a carpenter's apprentice. He was adamant he did not want the same for us.

He supported Prime Minister Errol Walton Barrow – "The Dipper" – and the Barbados Democratic Labour Party. He felt the previous leaders of Barbados had made decisions that benefited only the privileged white minority. He would say to me because of The Dipper, you can go to Harrison College, Lodge School or Combermere School. 'You don't have to be white or upper class to do so.'

* * *

Combermere School was initially established in 1695, 68 years after the island was settled, as the Drax Parish School, a "free school" formed by an endowment from the will of a former plantation and slave owner by the name of Colonel Henry Drax, ancestor of Tory MP Richard Drax, who inherited the Drax Hall Plantation in the parish of St George, Barbados in 2017. Colonel Drax's will of 1682 said: *Herein I give and devise for the erecting and enduring a Free school or College in Bridgetown, in the island of Barbados, to endure and continue for ever, to be paid by my Executors in England, three years after my decease, £2,000 ..... to the extent and purpose aforesaid.* The school, one of the oldest in the Commonwealth, went through several name changes and relocations, eventually settling on the name Combermere in 1819, after the colonial governor of Barbados, Field Marshall Stapleton Cotton, 1st Viscount Combermere.

The school's original mandate, back in the 17th century, was to educate the children of poor white families. The school, ironically, was also the first to offer secondary education to lower-class blacks on the island.

The Dipper, who started his secondary education at Combermere, democratised the education process and expanded free education to all levels, a victory against segregation in schools.

In 1975 I sat and passed the Common Entrance Exam for Combermere. Mum and Dad were the two proudest people in Barbados. However, even this meritocratic process was mired in privilege and entitlement. Several paid private primary schools would guarantee entrance into the top secondary schools. This guarantee was fraudulent, of course. It was accomplished by acquiring the actual Common Entrance Exam papers from the Ministry of Education weeks before the official exam and tutoring their pupils on those papers. This fraud was exposed in 1975.

Despite a merit-based Common Entrance Exam system in Barbados, most of the white minority population gain entry into the top four secondary schools. It can therefore be deduced that either the white population is more intelligent than the black population, or the system is manipulated.

At Combermere School, very early on, it was discovered that I had a talent for bowling a cricket ball relatively fast. Cricket at Combermere is played extensively, and the school has an exceptionally long list of former Test players. Sir Frank Worrell, Sir Wes Hall, and Sir Clyde Walcott started their secondary education there. Worrell was knighted for his services to cricket in 1964 and died from leukaemia at the age of 42 in 1967. A memorial service was held in his honour in Westminster Abbey, the first such honour for a sportsman. He was a *Wisden* Cricketer of the Year in 1951 and inducted into the ICC Cricket Hall of Fame in 2009. My own 1990 England tour of the West Indies included Gladstone Small, a fellow Combermerian, and the first black English Test umpire, John Holder, was also an old boy.

* * *

As my education and cricketing abilities advanced, Dad told me of the educational, sporting, economic and social inequalities that existed in Barbadian society. He told me that Belleville, Clermont, Crane, Rockley and Strathclyde were no-go areas for black people when he was a young boy.

One of his favourite stories was of Sir Frank Worrell buying the Welches Plantation House from Mr Pilgrim, a "High Red Man". After the sale had gone through and Mr Pilgrim had found out the buyer was Sir Frank Worrell, he was alleged to have said, 'If I knew the buyer was a black man, I would never have sold the house.'

He told me of the apartheid system that existed in Barbados club cricket too. The all-white clubs of Wanderers, Pickwick, Carlton and the black clubs of Spartan and Empire. Even the whiteness or blackness of these clubs was defined by class, with Wanderers the club for wealthy white landowners, Pickwick for rich white administrators, Carlton for "lower-middle-income whites and near whites", Spartan for upper-class blacks and Empire for lower-class blacks. Empire was formed in 1914 by a section of disaffected Spartan members after the Combermerian and future West Indies fast bowler, Herman Griffith was refused Spartan membership for being "socially inferior". Empire was refused entry into the Barbados first-division cricket competition on two separate occasions. Empire was eventually admitted in 1916 after a deadlock vote 2-2, with Wanderers and Harrison College voting for, and Pickwick and Spartan against. Arthur Somers-Cocks, Oxford graduate, teacher at Harrison College and later headmaster, as serving chairman of the Committee of Management, which considered Empire's application, broke the deadlock by supporting the new club.

Dad told me about the cricketer Robert Williams, brother of Cecil "Boogles" Williams, and later to be Chief Justice of Barbados Sir Deny Williams, who was refused membership of Carlton for not being "white enough". Cecil himself, a Carlton member, toured England in 1950 when West Indies achieved their first series win in England. One of ten siblings, Robert had a darker complexion and curlier hair.

He told me too of the Barbados fast bowler, Carl Mullins, who used to terrorise local batters at around the same time. When West Indies captain John Goddard, a white Barbadian, was asked why

189

Mullins was not selected for the 1951-52 tour of Australia and New Zealand, he was alleged to have said, 'We will not allow a black man to go all that way and knock down white people'. He proceeded to open the bowling on that tour with the gentle medium pace of Frank Worrell and Gerry Gomez. The Australian series was lost 4-1.

Dad also recounted a story of the 1954-55 Australian side invited to a reception at the Goddards' house. When the Australians arrived, none of the black West Indian players were present. In that West Indian side were the three Ws, Sobers and Clairmonte Depeiaza. The great Australian all-rounder Keith Miller is said to have asked where Weekes and Worrell were and was told, 'We do not socialise with the black players.' Miller allegedly responded, 'If Weekes is not here, neither am I,' and promptly left the reception.

This was the same series in which Dennis Atkinson and Depeiaza, at the fourth Test in Barbados, established a world record partnership of 347 for the seventh wicket. When Depeiaza reached his century, the crowd felt Atkinson had refused to shake his hand. There are divisions amongst the Barbadian public, whether this was a racist gesture or due to conflict over captaincy by the two Combermerians, Worrell and Atkinson. About 2,000 people had protested at the Kingston Racecourse against the appointment of Atkinson as captain for the fourth and fifth Test. At this point, the administrators of West Indies cricket were still of the opinion that the West Indies cricket captain had to be white.

Frank Worrell became the first black permanent captain of the West Indies in 1960 after a long campaign mounted by CLR James, then editor of *The Nation* newspaper in Trinidad and Tobago. Combermere School had thus produced the last white Barbadian and the first black man to be permanent captain of the West Indies.

* * *

Although throughout my early life, Mum had always preached to me, 'Life is not fair', and Dad had recounted various stories of injustices in Barbadian society. I had however never felt unfairly treated until, when I was 12, my dad asked what I wanted to do when I was older. I promptly said, 'I would like to fly aeroplanes'. His answer was a shock to me. He said, 'Black people don't fly aeroplanes.' Up to that point, it had never occurred to me that being black could stop you from doing anything.

* * *

When I won a scholarship to Malvern College as a 15-year-old, the headmaster of Combermere, Mr Charles Pilgrim, called me into his office and reminded me first of our school song "Up and On", based on a 1915 First World War poem by John Oxenham. The song was sung every morning at Combermere assembly and at the graveside of every fallen Combermerian. Pilgrim reminded me of my responsibilities to my family, to Combermere School and to Barbados. He told me, 'You will be a little black boy in England; you will have to work twice as hard to get half as far.' At the time, I thought, what is the old man talking about?

* * *

Having arrived at Malvern in April 1981, I was the only black boy in the school. Being the school's star cricketer and fast bowler, I was protected to a certain extent from racist taunts. Occasionally the boys would ask if people in Barbados wore grass skirts and lived in huts, and occasionally called me "chalky", "coon", "gollywog", "rubber lips", "Sambo", and "Sunshine". Of course, these words meant nothing to me at the time because they were not used in Barbados.

On the cricket field, there were a few occasions when I felt picked on. At Harrow School the umpire met me before the match and said, 'One short ball today and you will be off,' and at Repton School when my later-to-be Middlesex colleague John Carr was struck on the head, the match was called off. Was it to do with race, or just public-school rivalries?

* * *

When the conservative politician Enoch Powell, author of the "Rivers of Blood" speech, was due to address Malvern College, my housemaster Mr Duff had sought to ensure I was comfortable attending. He felt I might disagree with his views, but it was worth hearing them before deciding whether to dismiss them. I happily attended.

* * *

During the summer holidays of 1981, I played in the second XI for Worcestershire. I have a particularly vivid recollection of a banana being thrown in the match against Yorkshire at Headingley. I had no understanding of its relevance but noticed my colleague Dipak Patel becoming animated and going off to see the Yorkshire secretary. It was my first brush with overt racism.

* * *

Not all biases, prejudices or stereotypical views are based on race; some are based on ignorance. I remember suffering from a back injury and missing several games. During one exchange in the dressing room, opening batter Martin Weston said to me, 'You are a skiver'. I had never heard the word and was loath to ask anyone else what it meant, but I was determined to find out. So, I walked to the local library and found the answer.

* * *

Later, opening batter Tim Curtis had returned from his Cambridge University studies, and the club decided to sack second XI coach and captain Vanburn Holder and install Tim, alongside a few others, as second XI captain. From the beginning they showed a distinct lack of knowledge about fast bowlers and fast bowling but were locally born. And the best fast bowling coach in the club was lost to all of the young fast bowlers.

* * *

I was experiencing severe back pain, and during a second XI game against Gloucestershire at Bristol, so I informed one of the many captains of this fact. His answer was, 'If you are not going to bowl for me, you should fuck off', and asked head coach Basil D'Oliveira to

192

take me off the field. I was sent back to Worcestershire mid-match. I spent the next few days in pain but knew the club would expect me to represent my Birmingham League club, West Bromwich Dartmouth, at the weekend. I arrived at the County Ground on the Saturday morning and went off to see D'Oliveira to explain I would be unable to play the game. He said, 'For the good of you, me and this club, you should get yourself up to West Brom'. I was driven up, praying for the game to be washed out. Of course, the rain never came. I bowled one over, my back went into total spasm, and I was stretchered off.

After two nights in excruciating pain, my landlady Miss Collins decided to take matters into her own hands. On the Monday morning, I lay in bed and overheard her conversation with the Worcestershire secretary, Michael Vockins. 'This boy has been groaning in pain all night. If you don't take him to the doctor, I will, and then I am going to the newspapers'.

A specialist was hurriedly arranged, and by evening I was plastered from just below my neck to just above my private parts. I have great respect for John Elliott, the only member of the Worcestershire Cricket Committee who had the balls to call and apologise for doubting my genuine cry for help.

* * *

While some incidents can be attributed to a lack of education or to ignorance, some are arrogant, condescending and patronising.

I remember a conversation in the dressing room between John Inchmore, the Worcestershire bowler, and the great Pakistan all-rounder Imran Khan about the India and Pakistan conflict. Hartley Alleyne, the Barbadian fast bowler, asked what to him seemed an important question. Imran stopped mid-sentence and said, 'Hartley, if you have nothing important to say, don't talk'. It was the one time I felt like punching another cricketer in the mouth. It was downright disrespectful, arrogant and rude.

* * *

Sitting in the top-dressing room at New Road during a break in play, I could hear a commotion downstairs. As I got to the bottom of the stairs, I saw our South Africa-born England opening bowler rolling around on the ground clutching a broom as if it were a rifle. I asked, 'What on God's earth are you doing?' He said, 'I am showing the lads the combat positions we would take up while doing National Service in the South African army to shoot the blacks illegally crossing the border.' So, these absolutely desperate people in search of a better life were either eaten by wild animals or shot by the South African military.

* * *

One of the most shocking racist incidents occurred in the nets at Old Trafford. The nets were uneven, and all the bowlers were taking it easy. Our former England opener was batting. He turned to our captain Phil Neale and shouted, 'Tell your black c***s to bowl properly.' Instead of telling him not talk to his players like that, Phil walked over to Alan Warner and myself and asked us to please bowl the ball properly. Alan Warner's next ball struck the batter on the head. After recovering from the shock of the knock, he chased after Alan brandishing his bat. Alan, though relatively small in stature measured against the imposing batter, stood his ground and said, 'If you fucking touch me, you better never again fall asleep in the dressing room.'

* * *

During a period of a lack of opportunity, I decided I would make an application to the Royal Air Force. I travelled to the nearest RAF careers office to make enquiries. The young lady manning the office listened to my ambitions before asking if I had considered the army.

* * *

During another frustrating period at Worcestershire, I wrote a letter to the club chairman detailing my frustrations. When summoned to the committee room, I was under the assumption the contents of my letter would be up for discussion. In fact, all the chairman wanted to know was who had written the letter for me.

* * *

In December 1987 I was excited to be spending Christmas in Lyon with Kate and her family. On the night of the 22nd, her sister Sue phoned to advise the rules had changed and because I would be travelling on a Barbados passport, I would now need a visa. To add to the complications, the French Embassy would be closed on Christmas Eve for the Christmas period.

On the morning of the 23rd, I was first in the queue outside the embassy. As the doors opened, I walked to the booth and presented my documents.

The young lady sitting at the booth asked, 'What is your reason for travelling to France?'

'To spend Christmas with my girlfriend and her family.'

'How long will you be staying in France?'

'Ten days.'

'What is your occupation?'

'Professional cricketer.'

'What is to stop you remaining in France?'

'I can't because there is no professional cricket played there.'

'I need a letter from your employer confirming your occupation.'

'They are in Worcester.'

With a shrug of the shoulders, she returned my documents.

I walked out of the embassy disappointed. Suddenly I had a bright idea. I might be able to get the secretary of Middlesex to write a letter confirming my profession. Lord's was a short distance away, and I would soon be back in the queue.

Back, and armed with a letter just after lunch, I presented my documents once more to the same young lady. With a smile, she said, 'Ooh la la, there is no date.'

'Yes, but you remember I was here earlier, so the letter must be from today.'

'Sorry, I need it dated,' and she returned my documents with another shoulder shrug.

Ok. Second trip to Lord's. Soon I was back in the queue with a dated letter. Again, I made my way to the front and stood in front of the same young lady. She looked over the letter and smiled.

'Very good.'

And then, 'Ooh, la la.'

'What now?'

'The passport does not have enough empty pages.'

'You cannot be serious.'

'You need more empty pages.'

'How can I get more pages in a passport?'

'That's not my problem,' and she returned my documents.

I walked out of the French Embassy, totally dejected. Suddenly I had another bright idea. The Barbados deputy High Commissioner was a good mate.

'Hi, Owen, it is Ricky. Would you know how I can acquire some extra pages in my passport today?'

'Why?'

'The French Embassy says I don't have enough pages left in my passport for them to issue a visa.'

'You only need one page.'

'So I thought, but they need a few.'

'The French are so full of shit. Tell the guys at the High Commission to take a few pages out of an unissued passport and stitch them into yours.'

By the time I got to the Barbados High Commission on Tottenham Court Road, Owen had phoned ahead, and the pages were ready to be stitched into my passport. With my passport now carrying several new pages, I was back in the queue, but the embassy was now about to close.

I arrived at the front of the queue just as the guard said, 'The embassy is now closed.' In the background, I could see the young lady packing her stuff away. I waved, trying to catch her attention; perhaps she would take pity on me. She looked in my direction, shrugged her shoulders and disappeared into the back room. And with that, the guard shut the doors.

I travelled back to Belgravia, to the offices of Moët & Chandon, to give Kate the bad news. Sadly, we would not be going to France. I was in the stairwell of this great mansion building explaining to Kate what has happened and she was sobbing uncontrollably. Just then, a director of Moët & Chandon, Baron de Montesquieu, walked down the stairs and said, 'Joyeux Noël. Enjoy France.' And then he noticed. 'But why are you crying, Katy?'

'Ricky couldn't get a visa.'

'Non, non, non,' and with that, he turned on his heels and disappeared back up the stairs. It was now after 6pm and pitch black outside. Soon he was back. 'Go back to the embassy; someone will meet you. And have a great time in France.' We travelled back to Petty France and were met by the same security guard who had kicked me out earlier. He took my passport and disappeared inside. Moments later, he was back with my passport bearing a French visa on one of the original pages of the passport.

* * *

Moving to London at the start of the 1989 season was a new experience, both as a member of a multi-racial side and living in a massive city. In the Middlesex dressing room were Roland Butcher, Norman Cowans, Aftab Habib, Desmond Haynes, Mark Ramprakash, Paul Weekes, Neil Williams and Steven Sylvester. By and large, the dressing room was lively and boisterous but harmonious. You would hear the occasional stereotypical views. 'You black boys are all the same.' 'You know what you black boys are like.' 'You black boys always stick together.' It was the generally held view amongst the black players that none of us would ever be made permanent captain of Middlesex CCC, and only the white players would ever be employed by the club after our playing careers were over.

Paul Weekes would tell a story of football matches in his neighbourhood, Blacks vs Whites, but being of mixed heritage, he would be asked to referee.

* * *

The England players with West Indian heritage would all tell you how, in the British newspapers that when they did well, they would be known as "the English cricketer", but when they did poorly, they would be known as "West Indian-born or West Indian heritage cricketer". It was also felt that when England did badly, one of them would carry the can.

* * *

My fast-bowling colleague at Middlesex, Norman Cowans, had, I believe, made a calculated decision to prolong his career by throttling his pace

197

back from his early tearaway days. Even though he was undoubtedly as effective, he would be constantly called out by some of the white members of that Middlesex side as lazy. It was a widely held view by white members of the cricketing fraternity that bowling a cricket ball at 90mph by black fast bowlers was easy, and if a black fast bowler was not doing so, he was not trying. This view is still being perpetuated today by British cricket commentators about West Indian-born fast bowler Jofra Archer, whose dad Frank I was at Combermere with.

* * *

What I was unprepared for in London was the number of times the police would pull me over. Most were amicable, but on a few occasions, they were confrontational and accusatory. After some time corroborating my story, I would usually be allowed to go but was then often followed back to my flat.

On one occasion, I was driving Kate's mother's car, travelling home with my brother. I parked in front of my house, and a marked police car stopped in front of me, with another vehicle behind now flashing blue lights. Immediately, our car was surrounded by armed police, asking for ID, my address, and wanting to know who the car belonged to. Having cautiously given my ID, one of the coppers recognised my name. When the situation de-escalated, I asked him, 'Why me?' He said, 'Two black men in that calibre of car in this area will always attract attention.'

* * *

In sport, racism can be driven by emotions, ignorance, lack of education, and misguided enthusiasm. Usually, you can pinpoint the man or woman in the crowd using racist language. And usually, they do not consider themselves racist because they have black neighbours or their team has black players. In aviation, racism is more subtle, hidden, cynical and calculating. The main problem is the small gene pool, especially inside the flight deck. It is predominantly white males, who went to the same schools, the same universities, served in the military, with the same class and background.

* * *

Having given up professional cricket, I turned my attention to what was my first love, flying. Here was an opportunity to prove to my deceased dad that black people can fly aeroplanes. Very early on, I realised race would indeed matter when flight instructor Brynhilda at one school advised me, 'It is a fact that black people's brains are smaller than white people's.'

* * *

Having enrolled in the Oxford Air Training School in 1994 to study for the British CAA ATPL, several instructors repeatedly used the phrase, *a nigger in the woodpile*. Being unfamiliar with this, I sought clarification and was told it meant something that would catch you out. A "gotcha".

* * *

Having passed my licence at the first attempt, I started on the long journey of finding a job. I watched with envy as almost all my flight school colleagues got jobs. I wrote letters to pretty much every airline in the world. And the replies became known as a fuck-off letters (FOL) . I was offered a few interviews, but they all ended with a FOL.

* * *

One interview left a bad taste in my mouth. I arrived at Luton Airport half an hour before the scheduled interview and walked into reception. The receptionist seemed a little taken aback by my presence. I said I was here for an interview with the chief pilot. She immediately said that he was not in today. As I walked away deflated, her words just did not sit right with me. I decided I would position my car so that I could see the front entrance. Sure enough, the very same chief pilot soon walked out the front entrance. I chased after him and explained my position. Although he agreed to the interview on his return from lunch, about two weeks later, the company sent me another FOL.

* * *

Very early in my flying career at Virgin Atlantic, I became aware of some stereotypical views in the aviation industry. In one incident, I switched all the exterior aircraft lights on before doing the walk-around to check that they were working. However, as I walked around the aircraft, the lights were switched off. When back on the flight deck, I asked the captain why the lights had been switched off, and his response was, 'You people are so laid back; I did not think you would notice'. Being the first time we had flown together, it was an astonishing observation.

* * *

A first officer colleague was genuinely concerned about me operating with a particular South African captain, whom he felt was particularly racist. He relayed a story to me of a black cabin crew member arriving on the flight deck to advise this captain that push back would have to be delayed because there was no crew food loaded. As she left the flight deck, this captain turned to him and said, 'These people have only just stopped eating each other, and now they are worrying about crew food'.

* * *

On my very first trip to South Africa, whilst touring the township of Soweto, I asked the black tour guide how he felt about the white South African elite athletes such as Gary Player, the Pollocks, Barry Richards, Zola Budd and the like, who held great privilege under the apartheid system, now saying they disagreed with the system back then but continuing to reap the rewards even today. His reply, 'The whites of South Africa are like the person who stole your bicycle, says sorry, but keeps your bicycle.'

* * *

On 19 August 2001, I departed London Gatwick on the VIR15 for Orlando. The flight deck crew had been designated four nights in Orlando. The captain had brought along his son and was excited as the trip was like a mini holiday for them and on the 22nd there was a scheduled shuttle landing, which he was keen to observe. We were staying at the Orlando Marriott Airport, but with the captain spending time with his son and my crew returning to London, I was Ricky no mates. On 22 August, I was lying around the pool and my captain was at the Kennedy Space Centre. A young lady arrived beside my sun lounger and asked, 'Are you staying in the hotel?'

'Yes, of course.'

Moments later, she returned to repeat the question. On the third occasion I said, 'Yes, I am a Virgin Atlantic crew member.'

Moments later, two security guards arrived and asked me to leave the premises. I asked, 'Why?' One of them said, 'You were seen jumping over the fence, and now you are ogling these girls.'

I said, 'I might very well be ogling, but I certainly did not jump over the fence; there are alligators in that lake, for crying out loud!' He did not see the funny side, and became confrontational.

I thought this being America, with their gun laws, I had better leave the premises.

While I was being escorted through reception by these two heavyweights, I had a bright idea. Surely the receptionist would either remember me or have a list of crew names. So I ran over saying, 'I am Virgin crew, and I am staying in the hotel.'

'When are you leaving?'

'Tomorrow.'

'What's your name?'

'Ricardo Ellcock'. After checking, she said, 'There is no one staying here by that name.'

A booming voice came from behind, 'Now leave the premises and don't ever come back.'

Here I was, standing outside the Orlando Marriott. My captain was at The Kennedy Space Centre and I had no designated crew of my own yet.

I called Virgin ground staff at Orlando airport, asking them to meet me at the Marriott. After a couple of hours, the station manager arrived, and I was allowed back into the hotel, who were apologetic. On my return to the UK, I wrote to Virgin Atlantic to voice my concerns at the treatment I received from the Marriott. I am still awaiting a reply.

* * *

On a trip to San Francisco, the crew was staying at the Stanford Court Hotel at the top of Knob Hill. One afternoon, I walked down to Macy's in Union Square and was on my way back up Powell St, a very steep hill that plateaus several times during the climb, usually at a set of streetlights. As I started the climb, I was aware of a lady walking just ahead of me. At every plateau, we stopped to allow the passage of crossing traffic. At each of these stops, I was aware of her presence but not concerned for or about her. At the top of the hill, I turned left onto California St before turning left again into the Stanford Court reception area. As I approached the elevator, the door was open, so I speeded up to ensure I did not miss it. Suddenly the lady in the elevator started screaming,

'Don't rob me, don't rob me, take my bags, leave me alone, please, please!'

She was now bent over, cowering in the corner of the elevator and screaming hysterically. I was holding the door open, amazed. The concierge, having heard the commotion, ran over to the elevator.

He asked, 'What is the problem, ma'am?'

She explained I had followed her up the hill and was about to rob her. Luckily the concierge was fully aware of who I was, as we had often chatted in the lobby.

He said, 'He is a pilot who is a resident here.'

She was embarrassed and apologised but explained I had followed her from Union Square, and when she had turned into the hotel, I had done so too and had even tried to get into the same elevator. I accepted her apology.

* * *

As my Command course at Virgin Atlantic approached, I suddenly found I had to disprove any number of rumours, from being an alcoholic, smoking drugs, thieving alcohol from the aircraft bar, vacating the flight deck, failing courses, being awarded Command without an assessment, failing the assessment but playing the race card, and taking a ghetto blaster to work. Total nonsense, of course, but this was someone, or a set of people's, cynical attempt to derail my progress. Nevertheless, it resonated so much that one training captain promised to right the wrongs. Needless to say, whenever I saw him on my roster, I would swap or call in sick.

* * *

The training captain on one of my Command training details advised me during the briefing that it was his job to protect the Command seat. Even though it was company procedure for an abandonment of a take-off to be carried out by the occupant of the left seat, he said that in the event of an abandonment being required today, "he would be doing it from the right seat". It was a comment that made me wonder. Protect the Command seat from whom or what? And was this a comment used for everyone going through the course or reserved solely for me?

* * *

Virgin Atlantic Airways had started a pilot training scheme. With the cost of pilot training being £120,000+, it was a real opportunity for black kids, inherently the poorest members of British society, to become pilots. However, several years went by, and I did not see any black kids coming through the scheme. So I sought out the pilot liaison officer for the scheme and asked, 'Why is there a lack of minorities coming through?' He answered, 'Approximately half of the candidates are female.'

* * *

On my way home from university, a little old lady stood at the bottom of the stairs of Waterloo train station with four bags, wondering how she was going to get them to the top. I offered to help carry them and she gladly accepted. As we neared the top, she dropped her bags and dived at my feet and we both ended up on the floor. Lifting myself up, I said, 'Why did you do that?' Her reply, 'I thought you were going to run off with my bags.'

* * *

Being off sick, with a subdural haematoma, which required four operations to correct, did not prevent rumours being circulated by a few training captains at Virgin Atlantic of me drug-taking onboard and having to be restrained and removed from the aircraft. This was one rumour too far. I asked the airline management to advise the training department and the individuals involved to refrain from making false accusations, or I would be taking legal action. I am unsure if it was ever done, as I have yet to receive any feedback.

* * *

Over the years, being a black boy in a British public school, and a black man in two very high-profile jobs, I have experienced several racist events and plenty of racist language. However, the event that hurt the most was my 12-year-old son, who is of mixed heritage, with his mum a white middle-class woman from Staffordshire and me, a black man from a ghetto in Barbados. Isaac returned home from his British public school one afternoon to ask, 'Dad, why is it the bus driver always asks me for my bus pass but never asks for Benjie's?' I thought about going into the Martin Luther King Jr Promised Land speech or explaining the notion of working twice as hard to get half as far, climbing the rough side of the mountain, or just saying, 'It is because Benjie is white.' In the end, I just said, 'Issy, these things sometimes happen.'

ACKNOWLEDGEMENTS

To acknowledge each and every person who has made a difference would be impossible but there are some remarkable people who made a profound and long-lasting impact on my journey and for that I am eternally grateful.

Michael Clarke, my caring guardian, has been there throughout my life. He has been generous, compassionate and supportive and a major influence on the man I am today.

Alan, Sheila, Claire and Sue Duff, as well as Ann Collins, who treated me like their own. I will always be indebted for their love and kindness. RIP Alan and Ann.

Victor Sandiford and Ricky Harrison for gifting me the cricket equipment that started the entire journey.

Cousin Norma and Uncle Roy for the support they provided to Mum when we were suddenly fatherless and destitute.

Mr White, my Class 3 teacher, and Myrtle Nicholls, who gave me extra lessons. Both combined to help me pass the Common Entrance Exam.

Harcourt Wason, my Combermere games master, for giving me the opportunity to excel.

Andy Murtagh, master in charge of cricket at Malvern College for the support and guidance in the early days of my career.

School House Class of 1984 for welcoming me as one of their own.

Captain Bart Beelen, flying partner at flight school, for help and support during the course.

Dr Marie Toft for supporting me during my mental torture and sponsoring my plane ticket, enabling me to attend the LIAT interview. Hazel Mayers for feeding me at the start of my LIAT career when I could not afford to feed myself.

Zoral Bartley for the total support and help during my LIAT career.

Richie Kangoo for putting his own career at risk to help me attend my Virgin Atlantic interview.

Captain John Karman for his guidance, knowledge, leadership and patience during my Command course.

Professor Nigel Dennis and Dr Francis Kremarik for supporting me at the end of my MSc when I was ill. Without them, I'm not sure I would have completed the course.

Paul Newman for encouraging this project and editing the original versions.

My marriage to Kate came under strain with the stresses of flying, and our marriage sadly ended in divorce. We remain the very best of friends and as well as raising our incredible son she has been there in my most desperate times of need. Thank you.

My son Isaac for stepping up to the plate in my near-death situation.

Denise Doyle for saving my life with a timely call to the paramedics.

Lisa Halsey for coming to my rescue in my hour of medical desperation.

The Nigerian doctor at Frimley Park A&E, who used her instinct to go against the advice to discharge me. That instinct saved my life.